Praise for *Games at Work*

"What types of counterproductive games can you find in your organization? You are probably not aware of many of them, nor aware of the harmful long-term effects they produce. Reading *Games at Work* will increase your consciousness of the games played in the organizational arena and give you tips on how to neutralize them. An entertaining and insightful read."
—**Ney Simone Silva,** head of human resources, Camargo Corrêa—Engineering & Construction

"Goldstein and Read have identified a very important and overlooked area within organizations. Their analysis underlines how organizational games can undermine performance at both a personal and organizational level. Vigilance is needed if high performance is to be achieved."
—**Norman Walker,** senior advisor, TPG

"Outstanding way to describe in simple words and with a good sense of humor the real dynamics of corporate life. *Games at Work* is a must-read for newcomers and experienced people in global business who want to understand better how to identify and 'play' these unavoidable corporate games!"
—**Mauricio M. Adade,** president, DSM Nutritional Products, Human Nutrition and Health

"Deep insights into not only the corridors and meeting rooms but also the 'minds' of organizations! A must-read for everyone who wants to be aware of games played in big organizations but not necessarily abide by their rules."
—**Tarek Rabah,** marketing company president, AstraZeneca Pharmaceuticals, Gulf region

"An entertaining and practical tool kit for recognizing and correcting dysfunctional behavior in the workplace. With their vast experience working in many countries around the world and grounded in their rigorous research, Goldstein and Read serve as cultural anthropologists in credibly describing the games that the reader may never have noticed before and now recognize as true. This book is a must-read for all who are committed to improving the communications and culture of their organizations."
—**Tom Gross,** founder and managing partner, Genesis Consulting Group

"*Games at Work* will help you recognize and reduce the unproductive games employees play in your organization."
—**Eric Poll,** founder, OrgInt—Organisational Intelligence; former corporate vice president of human resources, Leica Geosystems

GAMES AT WORK

HOW TO RECOGNIZE & REDUCE OFFICE POLITICS

Mauricio Goldstein

Philip Read

Foreword by Kevin Cashman
Korn/Ferry International

JOSSEY-BASS
A Wiley Imprint
www.josseybass.com

Published by Jossey-Bass
A Wiley Imprint
989 Market Street, San Francisco, CA 94103-1741 www.josseybass.com

Jossey-Bass books and products are available through most bookstores. To contact Jossey-Bass directly call our Customer Care Department within the U.S. at 800-956-7739, outside the U.S. at 317-572-3986, or fax 317-572-4002.

Jossey-Bass also publishes its books in a variety of electronic formats. Some content that appears in print may not be available in electronic books.

Library of Congress Cataloging-in-Publication Data

Goldstein, Mauricio.
    Games at work : how to recognize and reduce office politics / Mauricio Goldstein, Philip Read. –1st ed.
        p.   cm.
    Includes bibliographical references and index.
    ISBN 978-0-470-26200-9 (cloth)
        1. Office politics.   I. Read, Philip.   II. Title.
    HF5386.5.G65 2009
    658.4'095—dc22

                                                                2008055669

Printed in the United States of America
FIRST EDITION
HB Printing 10 9 8 7 6 5 4 3 2 1

CONTENTS

For Larissa, Yoram, and Benny
For Diane, Danny, and Natasha

*G*ames *at Work* can change your life—personally and organizationally. As leaders, it is crucial to discern the art of
gamesmanship from the art of leadership. If we are equipped
to do so, authenticity and sustainable results will be ours;
if we don't, the results will be devastating for ourselves,
our teams, and our organizations. Understanding when we
are leading with character, serving all constituencies, and
when we are leading by coping, mainly serving ourselves
and our personal ambitions, is the essential key to moving
from self-focused to service-focused leadership. **Games serve
ourselves; authentic leadership serves others.**

Games at Work gives us the tools to become aware of the
games we all play. Why is this so important? Because without
awareness of limiting behaviors, we cannot rise above them.
While effective leaders elevate others to go beyond what is,
we first must become aware of what is holding us back. Read
and Goldstein give us the multi-dimensional resources to
elevate our organizations to go beyond gamesmanship to
authentic, value-creating leadership.

A while ago, I was advising a senior team in the midst of a
major crisis. The COO had made a huge, visible operational
error that the media was loudly clamoring about, and the
analysts were heavily punishing the stock. In response, the

COO put on his "game face." In an attempt to alleviate his fear of organizational and personal failure, his "let's look good" game kicked in. Presenting to the senior team, he painted a brilliant picture of the situation with impressive flair and analysis. He even identified a clear way out of the situation. The senior team was attentive and intrigued by the solution. You could hear a pin drop. There was just one problem—what he was saying was not true! Yes, it was a way out and, yes, it was tempting to the team, but no one said a word. Fortunately, the CEO stood up and with game-piercing directness said, "Bill, do you want to look good or do you want to make a difference?" Game over. In its place, a new pattern of behavior had been chosen: a choice for authentic conversations. The team mobilized around coming clean with the analysts and market about what happened and how they would not repeat their mistakes. The short-term result: the stock dropped even more and more courage was needed to stay out of spin games. The long-term result: the stock recovered and the company was repositioned for sustainable success. Trust and credibility were restored. The first step beyond organizational games had been taken.

If games in organizational life are so damaging, then why do they persist? Because they work. In the short term, people, teams, and organizations get what they want through games. However, in the long run, the cumulative effect of games can be devastating. Reducing games is directly proportional to improving organizational climate and increasing organization results. A leader who reduces his or her games becomes more authentic. A team that reduces games becomes more trusting and connected. An organization that reduces games becomes more believable, meaningful, attractive, creative, and productive.

Games at Work can literally transform individual, team, and organizational culture by reducing the life-draining aspects of games. Where do games come from? Why do they come up in the first place? Fear is the fuel of games. We unknowingly fill up the gas tank of game playing when we want something and are afraid we might not get it. Games are a way to cope with our stress in a reactive way to attempt to get what we want. Games are short cuts that don't get us to our long-term destination; games are a kind of labyrinth with no end.

Fortunately, there are effective ways to transcend games: courage, character, and constants, to name a few. Having the courage to express the right thing, the character to do the right thing, and the constants (values/principles) to know the right thing are the prerequisites to go from gamesmanship to true leadership. This is NO easy task. *Games at Work* is so important to organizational leadership because it gives you the understanding and techniques to actually accelerate these transforming practices in your organization.

Since games are inherently self-focused, they can have huge ethical downsides. As author John Dalla Costa in his work on ethics puts it, "Ethics in others." When John first shared this concept with me a few years ago, I thought it a bit simplistic, but as I went deeper into his core insight, I realized its profound simplicity. Leadership is the journey from self to service . . . the journey from coping to character . . . the journey from games to giving. When we are focused on authentic giving and service to others, games are perceived as superficial and self-promoting, both in ourselves and in our organization. Games are literally transformed through the alchemy of service and stewardship into a higher, more valuable mission or purpose. Moving our organizations from games to purpose is the real work of leadership.

Another dynamic that can transform games is awareness. We engage in games because we lack either an internal awareness of our fear or an external awareness of its impact on others. Engaging in games means our emotional intelligence is low. As Daniel Goleman, and others, has taught us, emotional intelligence is a heightened awareness of self and a heightened awareness of others, as well as the dynamic between the two. Emotional Intelligence reduces game playing and increases authentic human interaction. As Read and Goldstein so lucidly teach us, games must be significantly reduced to create organizations that are healthy organisms. If you put *Games at Work* into practice, you will increase the emotional intelligence and reduce the game playing in your organization.

Read and Goldstein have made a great contribution to organizational life with *Games at Work*. Imagine an organization with its energy fully harnessed onto leadership contribution, not diffused and distracted with gamesmanship. Imagine an organization focused on purpose, passionate about service, connected in relationship, and producing sustainable results. This is the world of work that *Games at Work* inspires us to create together.

February 2009

Kevin Cashman
Senior Partner
Korn/Ferry Leadership
& Talent Consulting

GAMES AT WORK

Introduction

In any organizational environment, people play games. This is true of even the most enlightened companies. It is in our nature as human beings to play games when we are in groups, when stress and anxiety exist, and when "prizes" (promotions, the boss's favor, funding for a project, winning a contract, and so on) are to be won and lost. It doesn't matter what size your company is or how it's structured. Although some cultures promote games more than others, just about every company possesses a game ecology—a pattern of games that form over time and that thrive in a particular environment.

Games take many forms and vary widely in their complexity. How people respond to them varies too: games can be positively reinforced, actively participated in, or minimized. Our purpose in writing this book is not to try to *eliminate* games. This is an impossible and, in a sense, inhuman task, akin to trying to stop employees from daydreaming. Instead, our intention is first to describe what we have learned about both the damage games cause and the benefits of reducing games, and second to share practical ideas for reducing them.

This isn't a theoretical study of game playing or a psychological treatise on the deeper needs being met by engaging in these activities. Instead, it is a practical guide to the world of organizational games, providing examples and analysis of the most common games played within teams and other groups as well as advice about the best ways to manage these games.

Before we explain how we became interested in this topic, we'd like to give you a sense of what a game looks like within an organizational context.

The Marginalize Game

Brendan was a twenty-seven-year-old whiz kid who worked at a top consulting firm. A Harvard MBA, Brendan was seen as someone who might become a future star. As a result, he was given a number of choice assignments early on, including membership on a new team that had been formed to analyze future growth possibilities for the firm. Brendan was the most junior member of the team by at least five years.

The Marginalize game was part of the firm's culture. Marginalizing was originally directed at poor performers, a none-too-subtle message that they weren't cutting it. Over time, though, it evolved and became a game used to isolate anyone who went against the group, who represented a threat from a job standpoint, or who made others uncomfortable because of his or her style or ideas.

Brendan represented a threat, so he was consistently marginalized by his colleagues and even by some of the younger partners. It wasn't that Brendan was arrogant or off-putting in his behavior, but he did challenge the firm's traditions with risk-taking ideas—ideas that other associates and younger partners saw as an indirect criticism of their more conservative approach. Even before this new team was formed, Brendan's colleagues had made his existence difficult. More than once, someone "forgot" to brief Brendan before a key meeting. When they went for lunch as a group, they sometimes didn't ask Brendan to join them, making a point of apologizing to him later for failing to include him (thus communicating that he had been marginalized).

On the new future growth team, the Marginalize game involved sometimes subtle but significant actions by other team members. For instance, Brendan received more than his fair share of low-level tasks, such as looking up articles and statistics—tasks that could easily have been assigned to someone in the research department. When Brendan came up with an idea that he was passionate about, team members grilled him mercilessly and nitpicked the idea to death. When Brendan complained about the way he was being treated, they talked to him about the need to be a team player and to learn to compromise—they marginalized him by making him feel guilty.

It shouldn't have surprised anyone when Brendan resigned to take a job with another top consulting firm ... or that he flourished in an environment where he was not marginalized.

Games: An Under-the-Radar Problem

Even Brendan might not have characterized his peers' marginalizing behaviors as part of a game. Few managers or employees would. They might acknowledge that they work in politicized environments where they must be savvy about how to get what they want—that a certain amount of manipulation and alliance building is necessary to get ahead and get what they want—but game playing is often a subconscious activity.

For this reason, it's a particularly dangerous and vexing problem. Games do their damage beneath the surface. They sap a company's people of energy and commitment. They lock people into routines and rituals that hamper flexibility and thwart change efforts.

If not for our particular backgrounds, areas of interest, and involvement with change efforts, we probably would have never identified these game-playing behaviors. We came up through the commercial, supply chain, and human resources functions at major U.S. and European multinational companies based in South America and Europe (Mauricio) and in Europe, the United States, and Asia (Phil), and shared an interest in what was causing productivity losses in organizations.

In 2004, as we were discussing this subject, we started to realize that beneath the surface of seemingly normal work activities, games were being played. We began describing some of these games to ourselves, and as we did so, we noticed that they seemed to echo some of the cartoons of Scott Adams. We asked ourselves, "Why do people laugh at Dilbert?" and understood that these cartoons often derive their humor from the counterproductive games people play in the workplace, as the cartoon on the following page illustrates:

This cartoon is an example of a game we call Token Involvement, in which a manager encourages his direct reports to participate with ideas and suggestions, but the encouragement is in fact a sham, as he has already decided what he wants to do.

DILBERT: © Scott Adams/Dist. By United Feature Syndicate, Inc.

As we reflected on our experiences and those of our clients through this game lens, we realized that people regularly exhibited "weird" game-related behaviors in organizations, and everybody considered them "normal" (and, in some organizations, they really are the norm). Clearly, these behaviors hurt rather than helped groups in their pursuit of objectives.

At the same time, we were fortunate to meet some leaders who neither played nor facilitated these games. They inspired and promoted open, productive, and creative behaviors in their people. Unlike these leaders, the majority of the people we observed and worked with were unaware of their unproductive behaviors and the negative impact they had. The more we studied these behaviors, the more we saw the gamesmanship involved: how there were winners and losers, how people were manipulated to gain an edge, how hidden agendas were behind what people often said and did. So we began talking about organizational games with others—with more than one hundred executives from different industries, different geographical regions, and different levels. They were intrigued with the idea and were curious about how to deal with these games effectively.

For the past few years, we've been collecting and analyzing our game data and categorizing games by type. We've also created a method that can be used for reducing the frequency and number of games, a method derived from our experience and from observation of individuals and organizations that play fewer games.

We'll be the first to acknowledge that our list of organizational games is incomplete and that our method isn't perfect. This is uncharted territory, at least from an organizational perspective. Some game experts (most famously Eric Berne) have written about this subject from the individual psychological standpoint. We, in contrast, have focused on the organizational perspective, looking at the games that emerge within typical work groups.

As we began working on this book and interviewing business executives, we quickly learned five lessons:

1. This topic is more controversial than we had initially thought; many people were unwilling to be acknowledged in this book and gave us interviews only under the condition of anonymity.

2. The notion of work games resonated with many individuals; people told us that this is "exactly what goes on" in their organization.

3. The loss of productivity caused by games is huge and hugely frustrating for many managers.

4. Everyone is complicit in games; game playing is a part of human nature, and although some people play harder and more often than others, everyone plays some of the time.

5. No one had any idea about how to get game playing under control; we discovered a deep sense of helplessness, as well as a strong propensity to blame people at the top for the situation (in a way itself a game).

This book is an attempt to explain games and then help you in dealing with them—personally, within a team, as a team leader, or even as the leader of a whole organization. The good news is that simple awareness and understanding of games have an enormously positive impact. Once you're conscious that they exist and you know what to look for, your odds of diminishing them increase significantly.

What This Book Will Tell You and How It Will Tell It

Expect to be educated and entertained. During our research and interviews, we learned a lot about this fascinating subject. We're going to pass on that learning in the form of organizational game descriptions, stories about games, and suggestions about what to do to reduce them (and what not to do). The stories we're going to relate are especially instructive, as they show how games play out in typical business situations: meetings, presentations, budget discussions, performance reviews, online communications, and periods of change. We did not name the companies where these games take place. We've also created fictitious composites based on real company games. We found that people didn't like to admit that games were being played on their watch; others were afraid that their employer wouldn't want them to talk about what was going on. At a time when increased productivity and growth are mandatory, game playing has especially negative connotations.

Chapter One defines common games and describes the traits which indicate that a game is being played. In Chapters Two through Four, we address the key issues surrounding games played at work: the impact games have on organizations, the environmental factors that make games so tempting today, and why individuals and organizations often ignore or downplay the negative impact.

Chapters Five through Seven offer a process for reducing game playing consisting of three steps: Awakening, Choice, and Execution (ACE). This process will help give you and your people the option of engaging in open, honest discussions rather than resorting to secretive, dishonest games.

Chapters Eight through Ten combine a broader organizational perspective with the individual manager's viewpoint. Although it's crucial for managers of small groups to manage the game playing within their area of control, it's also essential that leaders look at the impact of games on the entire enterprise. We'll focus on the ecology of games, the interlocking patterns of games that dominate different organizations. Next, we'll address a subject near and dear to our hearts: how game playing thwarts any type of change and what can be done to counter this effect. After that, we'll examine the role of the CEO and how what he or she does affects game management.

Chapter Eleven describes a company that has a very low level of game playing. What does such a company look like and feel like to work in? The description of Composite Corporation is built from the very best examples of departments and units we have seen in the real world.

As you move through these chapters, you'll find that games reveal how people misuse their time and energy to deceive, manipulate, and cast blame . . . and how they do so with great creativity and Machiavellian skill. No one is perfect, and games reveal the flaws we all possess. As we examine these flaws, we gain invaluable insights into human work behaviors.

Who This Book Is for and How to Use It

Whether you're a young professional just starting your career or a CEO at the top of an organization, this book is relevant to you. In our current high-stress and highly volatile environment, people are playing games more frequently and more intensely than ever before. If you don't understand what these games are and how they affect your group and your company, then you will be powerless to prevent them from having a negative effect. Therefore, this book is an educational tool, bringing you insight into why people play games and what these games involve.

Whether you are an individual performer, or have only a few people reporting to you, or you're running a company with thousands of employees, this book will provide you with a process for counteracting the impact of games on your particular group of people.

Whether you're an active player of games or merely a "bystander" (watching while other people play), the process for minimizing games is essentially the same. Obviously, if you're initiating or involved in games played in your company, you need to pull back from these behaviors. But even if you're not, the ACE process we share in the book's middle section applies. Awakening to games, making the choice not to play or facilitate them, and executing a strategy to substitute straight talk for games are what every manager and leader needs to do.

If you're an organizational leader, this book is especially useful. As you have grown in different organizations, you have no doubt witnessed many of the games described in this book. You may well have learned how to play certain games—or you may have learned not to interfere when others played them—in order to survive. That was fine then. Why isn't it fine now? Because we no longer have the luxury of wasting the time and energy that organizational games consume. Now, many organizations are fighting for their lives. Global competition, revolutionary technologies, scarce resources, widespread information, and many other factors have made it more challenging for organizations to be successful. On top of that, the increased stress and anxiety in the workplace cause more people to engage in more game playing than in the past.

Consequently, if leaders aren't aware of the impact of games and fail to take action against them, their organizations are bound to suffer the consequences.

We should also note that we've written this book for professionals across the world, not just in one country. We've spent our careers working in a variety of countries, and we've found that work games have no borders. Although the traditions and cultures of certain countries may influence the type of games played there, playing games is part of the human condition. We are reasonably confident that games are being played in the offices of the largest Japanese automaker as well as in a family-owned business in Scotland.

Our hope is that through a better understanding of games, you can improve the ability of your organization to reach its objectives, satisfy customers, and win in the marketplace, and, at the same time, contribute to making the working life of the people in your organization more fulfilling.

With that thought in mind, we'd like to introduce you to the world of work games and some of the ones that are undoubtedly being played somewhere in your organization.

CHAPTER 1

Let the Games Begin

What Games Are and How They Are Played in Organizations

Games would be easier for people to deal with if they were purely conscious activities, limited in number, and overtly played. Unfortunately, people are often unaware that they're playing games, and a variety of games exist, many of which are covert and subtle in nature. Thus an understanding of organizational games is essential. If you're aware of the particular games you or your people play and how they affect individuals and the organization, you're in a much better position to handle them. A lack of knowledge about games allows them to thrive. The more you know, the better able you'll be to limit their damage and turn the energy of your people in more productive directions.

Therefore, we want to focus here on helping you understand what an organizational game is and the common types. First, though, we need to define our terms.

The Theory and Practice of Games

At its most basic level, a game is a competition between two or more people in which the object is to win. No doubt, you've played board games, sports games, and the like, for which the rules of play are strictly defined. Games aren't always so simple or transparent, however. A branch of mathematics is devoted to "game theory," which was developed by John von Neumann in his book *Theory of Games and Economic Behaviour* ([1944] 2007, with Oskar Morgenstern). Neumann demonstrated that there was more to games than probability; he coined such terms as "zero sum games" and "payoffs."

Of greater familiarity is the work of psychiatrist Eric Berne ([1964] 1996), the founder of transactional analysis, who wrote the book *Games People Play*. Berne suggested that many social interactions revolve around games—that is, the interactions seem to be about one thing, but beneath the surface are concealed motivations and attempts to gain payoffs. Berne posits that these games are dishonest and prevent more meaningful ways of living.

In short, the mathematical and psychological theorists recognize that games are more than they seem, that they are often driven by hidden agendas and personal payoffs, and that they can do more harm than good.

Now let's bring this theoretical construct to life with the story of one particular game we observed being played in a large organization. The company had recently introduced a 360-degree feedback tool to foster manager development. Harold, a senior manager, received a significant amount of negative feedback from his team. Shortly thereafter, he contacted Stan, an HR executive in charge of the feedback program, and said he would like to have a meeting with his team. Harold explained to Stan that he wanted a better understanding of what behaviors he needed to change as well as more examples of behaviors that caused problems for team members. He emphasized that he wanted to communicate to his team that he cared about their feedback.

Given Harold's comments, Stan thought a meeting would be productive. Nonetheless, Stan insisted that certain ground rules be observed during the meeting, including refraining from defensiveness or accusations. Harold agreed to these ground rules.

When the meeting started, Harold was humble and polished, and seemed eager to hear additional feedback. People opened up and shared their concerns. As everyone talked about possible solutions to the problems raised, Harold became a bit defensive. Still, he seemed committed to implementing some of their suggestions until he mentioned that he intended to talk to the company's CEO, with whom he had a "close relationship," about what might be done about team morale. Then Harold said that it was too bad that a few people were spoiling things for the rest of the team. Immediately, a look of fear appeared on the faces of several team members; they clearly took this reference to mean that he intended to get rid of or move out some people.

After the meeting, Stan debriefed Harold about how things had gone, and Harold said the meeting was useful because "I figured out who was behind this, and that these individuals were a serious drag on department productivity because of their negativity."

In the following months, Harold created a tremendously antagonistic environment within his department, setting people against each other and focusing their energy on conflict rather than work objectives. Though Harold was eventually fired, his gamesmanship was very destructive.

The games Harold played included the following:

- *Token Involvement.* In this game, you pretend you want the input of others but are actually pursuing your own agenda. Harold suggested that he wanted to hold the meeting for the good of his team and for his own self-improvement, but in reality his goal was to identify people who were criticizing him, and he ignored the feedback.
- *The Boss Said.* In this game, you ally yourself with a powerful figure in order to intimidate others. Harold's reference to his close relationship with the CEO had this purpose.
- *Gotcha.* In this game, the goal is to catch and punish people who have "erred." Harold obviously used the meeting to figure out who was behind the negative responses in the original 360-degree feedback.

We should add that Harold may not have been playing these games on a conscious level; he may have initially wanted to use the meeting to become a better manager. Once the meeting started, though, Harold reverted reflexively to games he had played throughout his managerial career. In Harold's mind, he may have rationalized that he was simply protecting himself and his team from negative influences, but in reality, he was playing his favorite games.

The Traits: Signs and Symptoms That a Game Is Being Played

Defining something as a game can become a question of semantics. You can make the argument that just about any organizational activity is a game of some sort. When you take a few too many watercooler breaks, you're playing the "delay" game. When you spend one day working hard in your office and don't do your usual socializing in the hallway, you're playing the "turtle" game.

We don't define games so broadly. Or rather, our focus is on counterproductive games—those that drain people's time and energy, involve more than one person, and have ulterior motives and negative consequences for the organization. The following are the five traits that characterize these games:

1. *Manipulation.* People exhibit dishonest behavior to achieve their objectives. Sometimes this behavior is obvious and provocative; other times it's subtle. It may involve hiding information from a boss—telling only part of the story to make someone else look bad. It may involve making a problem appear more serious than it actually is, in the hopes of creating false expectations—the professional service provider who convinces a client that a goal is almost impossible to achieve, so that when he helps her achieve it, he'll come off as a hero. A person who is playing a game is not being straight; there is always some deceit and underhandedness.

2. *Paradoxical consequences.* Games often involve short-term gain for the player and short- and long-term losses for

the group (a colleague, the team, the department, or the company). For example, an individual plays a game to gain power over a peer, but most of his energy is focused on achieving this goal rather than on achieving a larger work goal. He may find himself being promoted and having power over his colleague, but he probably failed to take care of business on other fronts. Ultimately, he and the organization will pay the price for this neglect.

3. *Repetitiveness.* When certain behaviors become habits, they can also become games. For instance, most managers try to negotiate the budgets they receive from headquarters if they don't believe they are feasible. This is normal. However, when a manager believes that the budget is feasible, yet continues to negotiate budgets as a reflex or routine response, this behavior has become a game. When you always engage in a certain type of behavior in a certain type of situation, you're probably playing your favorite organizational game. Games create behavioral "grooves," and people become dependent on playing them and having people around who play the same games.

4. *Contagious effect.* Games are viral and thrive in certain cultures. In other words, games don't exist in one crevice of the organization and remain there. They spread throughout the company relatively quickly. We've seen such games as Sandbagging (managers knowingly low-ball sales forecasts as a negotiating ploy) spread with surprising speed, because when the game appears to "work" for one manager, others follow suit (and may even feel they "need" to follow suit just to survive and compete).

5. *Group activity*. You need two or more people to play. This is a crucial trait to understand, as the games you play will trigger the games your people engage in. They will follow your lead.

Games people play can be "interlocking"—that is, the game one person favors can fit nicely with the game a colleague enjoys. When people say that someone is a good fit with the organization or with a team, what they are also saying is that the individual's games interlock with the games played by a given group.

Beyond these traits, one frequent sign that games are being played is that everyone is pretending they're not. People are either in denial about games, or they've decided that the game playing is limited to a small number of highly political players. If you were to ask them if the majority of employees are distracted and diverted (from their tasks) by games, they would respond that goals are aligned, objectives are clear, performance is managed, and conversations and decisions are rational. They may admit that some political animals who enjoy manipulating others do exist in the organization, but they would rationalize that this is true of every organization and that these game players are a distinct and identifiable minority.

We should note that the prevalence and intensity of games played varies based on culture and situation. For instance, when a company's culture favors transparency, intellectual honesty, teamwork, and open debate, the prevalence of game playing is usually rather low. In contrast, fear-based, strongly hierarchical cultures, for example, tend to encourage game playing—people see game playing as the way to climb the organizational ladder, and fear that if they don't play, they'll be "losers." In these cultures, games become a way of managing the uncertainty and dependency that comes from being down the hierarchical chain.

Similarly, extreme short-term pressure and environments where disruptive change is taking place also tend to encourage games. In these situations, people use games to relieve the pressure as well as to deal with change; games provide an alternative method to deal with new people, policies, and processes.

Tangible or individually based activities also mitigate against game playing. When people are focused on creating program code or responding to a service center inquiry, for instance, they tend to work alone to achieve a clear, measurable objective. At the other extreme, project-based work, such as trying as a team to come up with a more innovative process to deal with slow customer service, can quickly deteriorate into a game; for example, team members waste energy on the Scapegoat game, scapegoating those who designed the original customer service process.

Now that you know the common traits of organizational games and the environment and situations that spawn game playing, let's look at our list of some more frequently played games and what they entail.

The Names of the Games: What They Are, How They're Played, and Why They're Harmful

What follows is a sample of some of the more frequently played games in organizations. (In the Appendix, you'll find a more extensive list of organizational games.) In every company, games will vary depending on everything from the corporate culture to work situations to personal proclivities. Nonetheless, the games on this list represent those that we have found to be played most often.

We've divided these games into three categories: Interpersonal, Leadership, and Budget. This division reflects the stakeholders with whom people tend to engage in games:

1. Interpersonal games—played with peers and bosses
2. Leadership games—played with direct reports and consultants
3. Budget games—played about the organization's money

These categories contain some overlap; an individual playing a Budget game may also be playing it in a leadership capacity; or a game that we've placed in the Interpersonal section may have an impact on budgetary issues. Categorizing is, however, a good way to get a handle on the main purpose of a given game.

Table 1.1 is the list of some of the most frequently played games, which we will describe in more detail, including examples illustrating the behaviors typical of each game.

Interpersonal Games

I1. Gotcha

In Gotcha, people act as if they receive points for identifying and communicating others' mistakes. This game is more likely to occur in companies that foster individual rather than collective recognition and that promote internal competition among employees to increase productivity.

TABLE 1.1: Frequently Played Games

Interpersonal	Leadership	Budget
Gotcha	Gray Zone	Sandbagging
Marginalize	Keep Them	Slush Fund
Blame	Guessing	Lowballed
The Boss Said	No Decision	Baseline
Big Splash Career	Token	Quarterly
Hopper	Involvement	Earnings
Victim	Kill the	
Gossip	Messenger	
No Bad News	Window Watcher	
Copy	Divide and Conquer	
Pre-Deal	Scapegoat	

Mistakes are seen as an opportunity to criticize others and put them down, and thus people hide mistakes rather than use them as learning opportunities. Also, any criticism will be seen as an attack, rather than as an opportunity for improvement.

Example: One CEO's favorite game was to go through "prereads" of presentations and try to identify the mistakes in advance. During the presentation, he would point out that "on page twenty-six, bullet point three is inconsistent with the data table on page seventeen." Even when the presenter was able to defend the inconsistency, the CEO would identify another and then another after that until he "caught" the presenter. Invariably, too much time and attention would be focused on analyzing the inconsistency, and the more important points the presenter was making were often lost.

12. Marginalize

In Marginalize, individuals are exiled from teams or groups because they challenge the status quo, aren't one of the boss's people, or don't "fit in" for other reasons. This game can be subtle or overt: leaving a person off distribution lists, not sending minutes to her, forgetting to call her. This cuts the person out of the decision-making loop and limits her effectiveness. People are often marginalized not because they're failing to contribute or are a drag on teams but for personal or political reasons. This game is often played in a passive-aggressive manner—for example, a manager gives a direct report a thankless task that prevents him from working on a mission-critical piece of business, but apologizes profusely for having to give him the thankless task, explaining that "you were the only one available to do it; I really appreciate it."

Example: The CEO of a food manufacturer had a favorite among her direct reports, a guy who was highly innovative and worked extremely hard. His peers, however, viewed this individual as the "teacher's pet" and played the Marginalize game by leaving him out of informal discussions, "forgetting" to invite him to meetings, and often ganging up on him when he presented a concept. It reached a point where it became difficult for this individual to communicate an innovative idea; he was discouraged despite working hard and continually met with resistance from his colleagues. Although this story may give the impression that the marginalizing efforts of these colleagues were obvious, the employees were actually quite clever in the way they played the game. In the CEO's presence, they seemed to treat this teacher's pet like everyone else. In private, however, they schemed against him in small but significant ways. Ultimately, he ended up resigning and taking a job with another organization.

13. Blame

In Blame, individuals point the finger at others in order to excuse their own behavior. For example, a manager may complain that he is not achieving successful results because top management allows the finance department to keep bureaucracy in the system. Blame can be placed on individuals, groups, events, or situations, but in all cases, it is part of a win-lose game where instead of engaging in an honest conversation or in a productive investigation of the real cause of failure, people devote their energy to setting up scapegoats and spreading word of their mistakes.

Example: When Costanza told Jack he was going to receive a smaller bonus than the previous year, she emphasized that she was at the mercy of the new human resources policy regarding bonuses, though she felt that Jack deserved a larger bonus. In truth, Costanza did have flexibility to give Jack a larger bonus, but she felt that Jack had not contributed as much as he should have during the past year and that a lower bonus was what was fair. At the same time, though, she didn't want to create tension between the two of them, so she blamed HR. This Blame game took various forms, including Costanza's continuing remarks to Jack about how HR was a pain and e-mails to Jack about other "wrong-headed" moves by the HR group. The game also took the form of Costanza's complimenting Jack excessively, as if her words were compensation for the bonus money Jack didn't receive.

14. The Boss Said

When playing the Boss Said, people invoke the name of a senior executive to help them get what they want or to add weight to the points they're making. They may make a request and imply that the CEO or some other executive wanted it done. In some instances, they may simply assume that this is what the boss wants. In other instances, they make it up. The game transfers power from the boss to the person who is making the request and using the boss's name. It often is played in cultures where communication is very formal and hierarchical, and no one would dare to raise a challenge or even to ask for clarification from top executives.

Example: See the description of Stan and Harold earlier in the chapter.

15. Big Splash Career Hopper

In this game, a manager new in a role develops a "big idea" (big splash) that will then be heavily marketed as both bold (entailing massive and rapid change) and successful (when judged in the very short term) and will justify his rapid promotion out of this job into another one (career hop), before the actual failure of this big idea catches up with him. In many instances the change is poorly thought through, and the concern during the change is less for the employees making the change than for the marketing and packaging of the change to the senior management (who may like the "ambitious" and "go-getting" tone of the initiative). This game can of course be played serially and constitute a significant part of a career, although it often catches up with a person when he has to remain in a position for a sustained period of time.

Example: Lydia, a manager of a marketing team, had been in position only a few weeks when she determined that what was really needed to "shake up" the team was a big drive on category management in a particular area. She spent a lot of time with consultants preparing the slides to sell to the global head of marketing, as well as effectively using all networking opportunities to pitch the initiative to other decision makers. However, she neglected to involve her own staff in this effort, and thereby missed some important feedback from the market that indicated that a different approach was required. Because Lydia had failed to communicate the rationale for the change to her team, they had no buy-in to the initiative. The change was pushed through (and a number of people who had real concerns that needed to be heard were sidelined as a result), and Lydia was able to sell the program as successful before it was really implemented. Lydia was soon in demand in another segment—she could "do the same for them"—and in less than twelve months, she had moved on before any tangible results of the program could be seen.

16. Victim

"I can't do anything because 'they' have made it impossible for me to do anything [by not recognizing me, by making stupid decisions, by promoting the wrong people, . . .]." This is the common sentiment expressed or thought by someone who plays the Victim game. Senior people may play this game by acting as if they're retired in place. Younger people may simply not work to their full capacity. No matter the age of the people who play the victim, they all spend a great deal of time grousing about why they can't accomplish what they need to accomplish and theorizing about the reasons for it. They often enlist others in these Victim game discussions, and it's easy for a victim mentality to spread and infect a team or other group.

Examples: Because the Victim game can be played in many different ways, we offer two examples here.

Max was a country manager in China for a pharmaceutical company. He had orchestrated the company's move to China two years ago and had set up operations in that company. The first year went much better than expected, but then a sudden downturn occurred for a number of reasons—increased competition from other large pharmaceutical companies, a quality problem with one of their products, the Chinese government's requiring significantly higher financial commitment from Max's company to operate in certain areas, and so on. Max responded by playing the Victim game rather than trying to fix the problems that confronted his company. He began spending an increased amount of time sending memos, e-mails, research, and other forms of communication to headquarters detailing all the factors that were affecting their group's performance. Max was tying up his human resources in justifying their failure in various overly detailed reports, the conclusion of each being that the China group was at the mercy of forces beyond its control.

In another example, Dennis, a thirty-five-year-old manager with a large consumer products company, was asked to join a cross-functional team assembled to help improve the company's knowledge management process. The team included relatively young managers from most of the company's functions—Dennis was in the corporate communications department.

The team was set up because the CEO was a proponent of knowledge management, and he felt that a great deal of organizational know-how wasn't being captured—or that if it was, it wasn't being disseminated to the right people at the right time. Dennis's team was supposed to work on ways to solve these problems.

Dennis had joined the company six years ago; it was his second job after having received an MBA. Initially, he was excited to be part of the organization, but in the last two years, he was twice passed over for promotions, and the boss he liked left the company and was replaced by one whom Dennis didn't like as much. More significant, the culture was somewhat politicized, and the people who did well tended to be those who were skilled at building the right type of relationships.

During the early meetings of the cross-functional team, Dennis didn't speak much, but when he did, it was usually to point out the inherent difficulty of making knowledge management a reality. He agreed that it was a great concept in theory, but in practice he doubted it would do the organization much good. Dennis wondered if their time was being used wisely. He mentioned that a few years ago he was part of another cross-functional team dealing with a diversity initiative, and described how they just spun their wheels and none of their suggestions were ever implemented. As the knowledge management team moved toward making recommendations, Dennis became more vocal; with regard to a given recommendation, he would ask, "Do you really think management is going to approve that?" Or he would warn the team not to make a certain type of recommendation because "it's too costly, and by recommending it, management will see it as an indirect criticism, since they've already spent a huge amount of money on knowledge management technologies."

Dennis managed to ratchet up other team members' sense of victimhood. People began relating their own stories about how the company (that is, a boss) failed to take a suggestion seriously or how they felt ineffectual in another type of situation. Eventually, the team reached consensus on recommendations that were perfectly acceptable and perfectly uninspired. By engaging in a multiplayer Victim game, initiated by Dennis, the team ended up opting for a "safe" recommendation rather than the recommendation they collectively thought was the best for the company.

17. Gossip

In Gossip, players use the rumor mill to gain political advantage. Most people are familiar with this game, as it thrives in volatile cultures—a good description of many organizations these days. The key component of this game is indirect communication. Rather than confront someone directly about a problem you're having with her, you talk to someone else and complain or talk negatively about this individual. You may also plant rumors that are designed to achieve some goal—keeping other people on their toes, sending a warning, sullying a reputation, and so on.

Example: A management team was discussing the possibility of promoting Sharon, a middle manager in finance, to a position where she would be involved in reviewing talent. During the meeting, Roberto, who had had a few run-ins in the past with Sharon, casually mentioned that Sharon wasn't really a "people person." He repeated this "people person" critique in a number of one-on-one conversations with members of the management team, passing on the rumor that a few years ago, Sharon drove an enormously talented man out of her department and that he landed at a competitor. As a result of Roberto's playing the Gossip game, the "not a people person" label stuck, and Sharon didn't receive a promotion she deserved—and one that would have benefited the company.

18. No Bad News

In No Bad News, players avoid or suppress negative data in relentless pursuit of a positive approach. This game can present itself in a variety of situations: avoiding giving someone negative feedback so his feelings won't be hurt; refusing to make a decision on the company strategy because you don't want to place higher priority on one area than on another; promoting a mediocre performer to another team so that you don't have to fire her; hiding poor results from a boss to avoid his wrath; and so on.

Example: Lucien sat down with Jean, his direct report, to discuss his performance review. Lucien was frustrated with Jean because of the latter's lack of initiative and effort. Lucien knew that Jean was smart and highly competent, but also that he was lazy. They had worked together for years, and Jean had always done a good job, but Lucien knew that he wasn't growing or coming close to his potential. At the same time, Lucien didn't want to hurt Jean's feelings, so he watered down his negative remarks to the point that they seemed minor. Although he told Jean that he thought Jean could work harder on some projects, Lucien added, "but I know you have a lot on your plate, and doing more than you're doing would be asking a lot." Lucien plays this same No Bad News game with his bosses as well as his direct reports, putting a positive spin on just about everything. The problem, of course, is that no red flags go up when problems arise, as Lucien disguises those problems through the game.

19. Copy

In Copy, the player sends paper or electronic copies to a boss, a colleague, or someone else who is not in the natural information loop. Copying can provide the copier with a sense of power. It can be used to communicate that the copier has clout. It can also be done to intimidate a third person, letting her know that a copy was sent so as to apprise the receiver of a given situation. Copying anyone outside the natural information loop automatically gets everyone's attention—it can be used for multiple purposes, including offering documentation in case something goes wrong. The key, though, is that it is a sneaky form of communication, one that's done with ulterior motives. It creates suspicion and distrust, as everyone knows the copier has a hidden agenda.

Example: Tojiro copied four different executives in his e-mails whenever he made a decision that entailed some risk. Tojiro, a young executive with a financial services firm, played the Copy game with an eye toward protecting himself in case any of his risky decisions didn't pan out. Because his company's culture was highly results oriented and political, Tojiro saw this game as nothing less than self-preservation. The Copy game was widely played at

Tojiro's company, and people seemed to think that as long as they covered themselves by copying, they wouldn't get hurt if a decision turned out badly. This wasn't the case—the culture was highly punitive—but people comforted themselves with the illusion that if they copied, they would be safe.

I10. Pre-Deal

In Pre-Deal, the player pretends that all the issues will be discussed in a meeting with persons x, y, and z, but in the meantime makes a pre-deal with a power broker in the organization, and the whole thing is a fait accompli. This is a classic meeting game, one that gives meetings a bad name. People spend hours and hours meeting, but it's all just for show, because one person has an informal agreement with a key decision maker in the organization, and the other people in the meeting are in the dark about this deal.

Example: Margie had what she thought was a terrific way for her group to reduce costs, but she knew that if she presented it during the monthly meeting of the company's financial group, it would engender endless debate and would take a long time for everyone to reach consensus. For this reason, Margie approached the CFO prior to the meeting and explained her cost reduction plan. The CFO liked the idea, and he agreed with Margie that if she were to present it during the next scheduled meeting, it could take weeks or even months before all the objections to it could be addressed. Therefore, the CFO asked Margie not to present the idea during the meeting; they would simply talk about the usual cost-cutting options. After the meeting, the CFO would announce that he had come up with a cost-cutting solution and that Margie would be in charge of implementing it.

Leadership Games

L1. Gray Zone

In Gray Zone, players deliberately foster ambiguity or a lack of clarity about who should do what. The purpose of this game is to avoid clear accountability. It can also be used to create tension between direct reports or departments, resulting in uneasiness that spurs people to work more productively. The Gray Zone game also may provide managers with ways of avoiding conflict with their direct reports; rather than decide something that upsets direct reports, managers operate indecisively and therefore don't clash with their people. Gray Zone may have the benefit of increasing productivity or avoiding conflict in the short run, but this game is the enemy of effective execution in the long run. When people aren't clear about what their roles should be, they perform them poorly; further, the roles aren't linked to organizational goals.

Example: Steve was a senior leader at a large organization with a traditional structure and a manufacturing base. The company was evolving, however, and as it began outsourcing many of its manufacturing operations, it also began restructuring in order to become a faster-moving, more adaptive company. Steve found that as they moved to a matrix-like structure, a number of tension points arose between himself, his direct reports, and his colleagues in other functions. To diminish this tension, Steve played the Gray Zone game. He took advantage of the new, looser reporting and decision-making structure to avoid making clear choices about who was responsible for what project. He would frequently tell his team, "We're all responsible for getting this done," without ever making anyone accountable for a project's completion. In this way, Steve didn't step on anyone's toes, and no one felt slighted or ignored. Of course, relatively little was accomplished in the area for which Steve was responsible.

L2. Keep Them Guessing

In Keep Them Guessing, the player changes her mind on key issues, without acknowledging that she previously had a completely different view or allowing anyone to point this out. People never know which way a manager's mind will go, and so become very cautious in their presentations and recommendations. Some top managers play this game because they want to be viewed as flexible, yet they fail to recognize the cost of hyperflexibility. When no one is sure what a leader believes or wants, confusion or even chaos is the result. People devote themselves to trying to anticipate what a leader requires rather than acting with a sense of purpose and shared mission. Flexibility must be balanced with clear goals and processes, and managers who opt for Keep Them Guessing rather than clarity will lower their group's morale and diminish their output in the long run.

Example: Marianne, an ambitious thirty-three-year-old manager in a relatively young, rapidly expanding organization, wanted to be seen as someone who was highly adaptable—this was the CEO's credo. Consequently, Marianne was quick to note which way the wind was blowing and to move in that direction. She kept an eagle eye on trends and industry events, and every new change in the field influenced how Marianne viewed various policies and practices. Her people, though, were bewildered by her sudden shifts. One day Marianne favored an aggressive policy toward customers; the next she advocated a more cautious approach. Even worse, one day a direct report would go into Marianne's office and ask her how she wanted him to approach a particular customer with a problem, and she would respond in a particular way. A week later, another customer would have a similar problem, and she would offer advice to a direct report that was quite different than what she had provided the first person who asked for help. Direct reports would compare her advice, scratch their heads, and spend a lot of time trying to "read" which approach Marianne favored.

L3. No Decision

No Decision involves finding innumerable reasons not to make a choice. Some of these reasons can make sense on the surface, but the underlying reason for playing this game is that if you don't decide, you can't be punished for making a bad decision. The impetus for playing the No Decision game can come from a variety of sources: people are new to the function or business and don't trust the information they receive; they come from a slow-moving industry where there was more time to make decisions; they are intimidated by a chaotic, fast-moving environment and believe they'll be "safe" if they avoid deciding. Players of this game are often skilled at looking as if they're simply being cautious and are focused on making the right decision slowly. In reality, they are creating task forces, holding meetings, issuing white papers, and creating the impression that they're taking action while in reality they are simply biding their time.

Example: A key position opened up at a major packaged goods company when an A player product manager decided to leave and join a competitor. This was a big loss for the company, and a lot of debate ensued among senior leaders about why he had left and what they might have done differently to keep him. The CEO weighed in and said that it was critical they replace the departed manager with an equally skilled individual and make sure they kept him in place for at least five years. The HR vice president in charge of the search to fill the position started the process by interviewing others in the organization and trying to identify the right specs for the job. Then he began assessing whether any internal candidates existed who met the specs. When he determined that none did, he began looking outside for a qualified candidate. Unfortunately, he couldn't find anyone who was a "good fit." Ultimately, he recommended that the organization split the responsibilities of this unfilled position among three other managers and renew the search in six months to see if a good candidate could be found then.

The HR vice president was playing a version of the No Decision game, making a good show of doing things while knowing that the safest thing to do was nothing (as filling the position with the wrong person or at least one who wasn't as good as the previous job holder was a distinct possibility).

L4. Token Involvement

To play Token Involvement, a manager conducts opinion surveys, focus groups, or involvement meetings to communicate that "your opinion matters," but these activities are done only to make people *feel* involved rather than actually to involve them. The real intention is just to get rid of the complaints and for managers to show their management that they're doing the "right" thing—involving their people in the decision-making process. The same game is played when leaders involve their direct reports superficially, soliciting their views on department strategy but relying exclusively on their own view. Cynicism becomes employees' ultimate response to this game, and they lose respect for management. Perhaps even worse, when management really needs employees to be committed and contributing to a major project, they have great difficulty securing this involvement.

Example: Dan has responded to his new boss's belief in "participatory decision making" by holding weekly meetings with his staff, during which he encourages discussion of the issues facing their group and requests their ideas. A secretary records everyone's ideas and creates a report, which Dan says he will incorporate into his decision making. After making a decision, Dan always thanks certain members of his team for their contributions and emphasizes that the course of action chosen was influenced a great deal by their participation. He also sends an e-mail to his boss extolling the contributions of these individuals.

In reality, Dan always does exactly what he wants to do. He may even sincerely believe that he has actually listened to the ideas of others and integrated them into his decision, but it's clear that he has certain biases and that he always follows these biases when opting for certain tactics and strategies, regardless of the information and concepts others bring to him.

L5. Kill the Messenger
Killing the messenger is an ancient tradition: you take out your frustration on the people bringing you bad news, rather

than on those who have created it. This is a game of kings, and it is also a game for leaders who lack a tolerance for negative information. Being able to absorb and learn from negative events is a critical skill for leaders today, yet rather than develop this skill, they play Kill the Messenger. The end result of this game is that people filter their reports to the boss, taking out any reportage that might engender an outburst. These leaders then operate from an unrealistically optimistic perspective; they think things are going great and are unable to plan for downturns or competitors' moves.

Example: Forbasaw, a senior vice president with a marketing services agency, played Kill the Messenger whenever one of her people would tell her something about the firm's clients that she didn't want to hear. Instead of listening quietly and analyzing objectively, she would always respond with an accusation along the lines of "The bad news you're telling me is a result of your not staying on top of the account." In other words, Forbasaw couldn't accept that clients would be unhappy for any reason except that their representative was doing a bad job. Of course, her people learned not to communicate clients' unhappiness, so Forbasaw operated in a blissful bubble, thinking that everything was going fine when in fact there were serious problems with a number of clients but her team was now playing No Bad News.

L6. Window Watcher
The boss doesn't want to fire someone (for financial reasons, for fear of lawsuits, or because of the possibility of some other form of unpleasantness), so he promotes her or moves her to a non-job (a role the Japanese sometimes refer to as window

watching), therefore removing her from a position of influence. This is why some companies are filled with "deadwood"—people who keep jobs for years and never really accomplish anything, but don't rock the boat. The Window Watcher game has a tremendously negative impact on productivity, an impact that is often invisible because the individuals given nonessential roles appear to be contributing employees. Part of the Window Watcher game involves creating the illusion that these people are still active, useful members of the organization while shuttling them to the side.

Example: Jim was a recently hired executive with a midsize leisure products manufacturer, and he came from a smaller organization that had been financially devastated by an employee discrimination lawsuit, filed by a woman who claimed she was denied promotions because she rejected a boss's romantic overtures. Jim believed that the boss had not made these overtures and that the woman had fabricated her story, but it caused him to play the Window Watcher game at his new company. In this instance, Sara, one of the direct reports he inherited, was sixty-two years old, and Jim thought that she wasn't pulling her weight. At the same time, Jim viewed this employee as potentially vengeful and didn't want to fire her and risk a lawsuit. Jim assigned her to a project that would take over a year to complete and removed her from the day-to-day operations of Jim's unit. To make this move happen, Jim had to spend a lot of time convincing his own boss that Sara had the skills that were necessary to the project, and he had to fill out a great deal of paperwork generated by HR. Even worse, it left Jim one person short of a full team, negatively impacting their productivity.

L7. Divide and Conquer

In Divide and Conquer, the boss deliberately pits subordinates against each other in order to maintain or consolidate power. The boss may also divide what his subordinates control, reducing their staffs, their sales territories, or their responsibilities in order to prevent a challenge to his influence or even his job.

Example: A CEO was concerned about the potentially powerful alliance between the head of Research and the head of the company's main division. She instructed the head of Research (who reported to the division head) to have weekly one-on-one conversations with her, and insisted that he was not to share the substance of these meetings with the division head. The CEO knew that word of these meetings would reach the division head and that it would create a wedge between the division head and the Research head.

L8. Scapegoat

Scapegoat is a bit different from the interpersonal Blame game, in that when leaders scapegoat, they do so to avoid taking the heat for an organizational program that is in trouble (rather than as a way to target an internal rival). Many times, managers set up consultants as scapegoats, communicating that a project's demise or a strategic misstep was the fault of a consultant who was involved with it in some way.

Example: A productivity program was successful (in the sense that the target numbers were exceeded) but hugely unpopular in a global consumer goods organization. One of the Big Five consulting firms had been brought in to orchestrate the program. The CEO was happy to take the savings the program produced, but he was not willing to accept responsibility for how the program hurt morale and resulted in the loss of some key personnel. As a result, the CEO fired the consulting group, maintained that their recommendations resulted in the morale problems, and hired another consulting group to investigate the "misdeeds" of the first one.

Budget Games

B1. Sandbagging

Sandbagging is played in two forms: by managers who have a P&L responsibility and by managers who have cost center responsibility. In the first case, managers purposely lowball sales forecasts as a negotiating ploy. Headquarters, knowing that this is a common practice (as they themselves were managers before and used to play this game), engage in a sequence of negotiations, losing trust in their managers' real judgment and often coercing the managers to accept a top-down number at the end of negotiations. In the second form, managers purposely present a higher budget than actually required, to start negotiations. This game creates "victimized" managers who don't feel totally accountable for the budget and may even try to demonstrate that they were right in the first place.

Example: Paolo, a very experienced leader, now the country manager of a global generics company in Russia, realized that the country generics market was booming and that he could easily grow sales by more than 70 percent the following year. Of course, it was still an unstable business environment, and any new government regulation could cause an abrupt slowdown in marketplace growth. He had also seen what happened to a colleague who delivered sales growth that was "below expectations" (despite all his efforts).

Paolo presented a modest forecast including 25 percent growth, much above the average 15 percent company growth, but below his real potential. After some back-and-forth with his boss, the head of emerging markets, they agreed to a forecast of 35 percent growth, which Paolo exceeded by 5 percent. His achievement guaranteed a fat bonus for him and his team, but it was much below the 70 percent he could have gone for.

B2. Slush Fund

To play Slush Fund when discussing the following year's budget, a manager mislabels one section, creating a secret surplus to cope with overspending. The problem with this game is that it encourages managers to play fast and loose with their budgets, draining money from the corporate coffers that they might not need. It also sets a bad precedent, communicating that budgets are not to be taken at face value and that playing games with them isn't just optional but necessary. Management eventually begins to suspect that managers are playing this game, and they begin questioning every line item in the budget, wasting enormous energy debating with managers whether item x is really necessary. Sometimes the slush fund even needs to be spent unnecessarily just to avoid questioning.

Example: Marcia, a midlevel manager at a consumer electronics company, routinely included an item in her budget labeled "special projects." Although Marcia would occasionally have a special project for which she needed money, she always allotted more money for special projects than she anticipated requiring. She rationalized this game by telling trusted colleagues that if she didn't have this slush fund, she would invariably go over budget, be chastised by her bosses, and be told that she needed to do a better job of watching her spending. "My way," she said, "I stay in management's good graces and make sure my department is properly funded."

B3. *Lowballed Baseline*

In Lowballed Baseline, a manager steps into a new role—after joining the company or after being transferred or promoted—and immediately starts telling people that the department is in bad shape financially. By disparaging his predecessor, he sets low expectations that he is able to meet or exceed, thus appearing to have "turned things around." Some managers are highly skilled at playing this game, shading the facts just enough that their pessimistic projections feel accurate. They may well enlist others in this game, encouraging their direct reports to help them slant the facts negatively. A great deal of effort goes into creating this low baseline, and therefore not much effort has to be expended on actual work, as anything above the baseline will be considered a success.

Example: Elena was a new manager who joined a company that had just gone through an acquisition, and she was given a position of responsibility within the acquired group. Elena declared that the unit was a "mess"—that given its structure, its personnel, and its products, there was no way it could come close to the CFO's financial projections for it. She seized on one negative factor—that a few people resigned after the acquisition—and talked about how these were "indispensable" individuals and that the loss of their knowledge and expertise would make it impossible to operate effectively until new people were hired and trained. In fact, the people who left were B and C players, but Elena did a masterful job of portraying them as A players.

B4. *Quarterly Earnings*

The Quarterly Earnings game is the attempt to meet the analysts' collective expectations or exceed them by only a penny in terms of quarterly earnings. This game produces a lot of decisions about what to book or not in a quarter and what to actually do in a quarter. (It also spawns a lot of other budget games.) As a result, organizations focus a great deal of time and effort on delivering the results that are right for analysts rather than the results that are best for the organization.

Example: Abbud, the country head of a cosmetics company in Peru, was promised a huge stock option grant if his organization achieved the sales growth estimated for the year. Unfortunately, November coming, Abbud realized that he was going to run short of the target by 5 percent. He called Jordan, his head of sales, and instructed him to negotiate a special discount with a few key customers if they agreed to buy 25 percent more than their average order. Playing the Quarterly Earnings game, Abbud achieved his target and compensation, at the expense of the company's profitability and the following year's first-quarter sales.

A Range of Attitudes: Game Consciousness

Don't assume that everyone plays these games with the same mind-set. Whereas some people are fully aware that they are engaged in manipulative behaviors whereby they win and others (including the organization) lose, in many cases they have little or no consciousness that they're playing games.

Even when they have been playing these games habitually for years, they wouldn't categorize their behavior as having anything to do with games. Typically, people with relatively low game consciousness only "glimpse" the game. It is difficult to glimpse a game if it involves behaving in a way that is similar to how they've acted all their lives. For instance, if they've always been a nitpicker and a finger pointer, the Gotcha game will feel like second nature, and they won't identify it as a game. If, in contrast, they have always been loath to point out people's mistakes and this is a game that is popular at their organizations, they are much more likely to glimpse it. They may not tell themselves they're playing a game, but they will be aware that they are engaged in an uncomfortable pattern of behavior endorsed by a company's culture.

People who receive and are receptive to feedback are more likely to have higher game consciousness. Your direct reports are especially attuned to your behaviors, and if you create the right environment for them to give you feedback, they will tell you if they perceive that you're afraid to say anything negative to them about their performance (No Bad News game) or that you reflexively copy other executives on e-mails (Copy game). If you encourage and listen to this feedback, you're likely to be a self-aware individual who knows the games to which you are vulnerable. This is one of the ways in which companies can start to mitigate game-playing behavior; we will look at others later in the book.

Understand, too, that game consciousness tends to be a reverse evolutionary process. By this we mean that when people join companies, they are often highly aware of the new ways of doing things in their particular companies, and they know that these norms are different from what they're used to.

In their own minds, they see a particular new behavior as a way to get ahead or play politics. Over time, however, this behavior becomes the norm, and their awareness that they're engaged in a type of game diminishes. They essentially are absorbed into the new culture.

The same holds true for veteran employees who find themselves with a new boss or CEO who introduces new elements into the culture; at first these "foreign" ways of doing things may appear game-like or overly political. Again, over time, playing these games becomes the norm, and people lose their awareness of them.

In any company, a small group of people exists on each of the far ends of the consciousness continuum. On one end, there are a minority of Machiavellian types who relish manipulating others, suboptimizing their groups for their personal gain, and making a given game or games habitual behaviors, all the while believing that this is just corporate reality. On the other end are people who abhor games, who are constantly looking for ways to improve, and who would rather resign than stay in an organization where games run rampant.

The majority of employees, though, are in the middle of the continuum, glimpsing that they're sometimes engaging in games but not fully aware of that fact.

The person who is on the game-conscious end of the continuum is unusually transparent and authentic. What you see is what you get. Rarely does this individual have hidden agendas. She possesses a genuine quality that invites trust and open communication. When she wants direct reports to work harder or better, she doesn't resort to the manipulative actions that are part and parcel of all games. Instead, she attempts to rally them around a worthy cause or objective, using her passion and commitment to encourage others to excel. She is not averse to asking for help when she needs it or admitting her own fears and doubts when she has them.

Although it's possible that this manager may unknowingly be drawn into a game others play, she won't play it for long. As soon as she becomes aware of what she's doing, she'll disengage or at least try to manage this behavior. She takes pride in choosing how to behave in a given situation rather than being controlled by the game routine.

In an article titled "Level 5 Leadership," Jim Collins (2005) suggests that great leaders combine "humility and fierce resolve." These are apt terms for leaders who avoid game playing. Their humility prevents them from resorting to games to flex their position power muscle or achieve personal goals at the expense of organizational ones. At the same time, they achieve great things through inspiration and perspiration rather than manipulation. This approach has a positive impact on both people and organizations, unlike game playing, the negative impact of which we will discuss in Chapter Two.

CHAPTER 2

Playing to Lose
The Negative Impact of Games on Core Business Activities

Games are insidious. By that we mean that the effect isn't always obvious and immediate. On the surface, short-term results may be good. Beneath the surface, however, problems are emerging. As a manager, you can glimpse some of the problems. You may notice that your people aren't bringing the same enthusiasm and energy to tasks that they once did. You may suspect that the "wrong" people are being hired and promoted. You may find that a key direct report resigns unexpectedly.

Taken as isolated incidents, none of these are particularly alarming. It's only when you notice that the impact is spreading and intensifying—that it is diminishing your group's productivity in ten different ways—that it dawns on you the damage games can cause.

To give you a sense of the impact of games within a group, we begin this chapter with a story of one team that played Gotcha too long, too hard, and with disappointing results.

A Finger-Pointing Environment

Tim was the head of a recently formed cross-functional team in a large, sales-driven organization. Tim's company had a reputation for a high-risk, high-reward culture; people who performed superlatively were handsomely compensated, whereas those who delivered average or even slightly above-average results usually departed relatively quickly. A great deal of internal competition existed for top jobs, and the company attracted highly competitive individuals who enjoyed the infighting for resources and promotions.

Tim's team was formed to address a customer service problem, one that involved slow turnaround times in response to requests for technical support. Representatives from sales, manufacturing, finance, and HR were on the team. Tim was a senior vice president of sales, and he was named the team head because of his ability to deliver results and drive others to perform.

Although Tim had a number of strengths, he was not particularly well attuned to the games his people played. Gotcha was played frequently, with team members reflexively pointing out mistakes and arguing about them in team meetings. At times, Tim felt like a referee rather than a team leader. As his team worked on resolving the customer service issues, they hit a number of walls in their attempt to come up with a solution. When they hit these walls, team members wasted time pointing out how Joe messed up or how Jill failed to acquire the necessary support from her group. Many times, team members would take Tim aside and explain how if he replaced Joe with someone from another group, the team would function that much better and would no longer have to deal with Joe's mistakes. The Blame game, therefore, was played in conjunction with Gotcha.

The team had launched with a great deal of enthusiasm and energy; being on this high-powered team was considered a plum assignment. Team members were eager to offer ideas and do the work necessary to explore them as possible solutions. Within a month or two, though, people began playing it safe. After having their mistakes highlighted by fellow team members as well as by Tim—and after being blamed for the team's slow progress toward dealing with the customer service issues—they lost their initial momentum. Team members did their work by the numbers, keeping a low profile and never suggesting any fresh ideas that might expose them to criticism.

Tim was aware that the team had lost its momentum, that they were dragging their feet in terms of coming up with a recommendation, and that their ideas weren't particularly innovative. What he wasn't aware of was how the Gotcha and Blame games were hurting morale, creativity, and execution. When the team finally reached consensus on a recommended strategy for solving the customer service problem, it was uninspired; the executive committee recognized this and disbanded the team.

As smart as Tim was, he didn't recognize the games for what they were. To him, the finger pointing was just par for the course—he was savvy enough to know that people got ahead in the company by playing politics. He rationalized that there was nothing terrible in pointing out mistakes; if you didn't identify what was wrong, you couldn't do it right the next time. Tim failed to connect the dots. Even if on some level he understood that his team members were engaged in Gotcha and Blame, he didn't see the impact of these games. As a result, he did nothing to mitigate that impact.

The Four Effects of Unmanaged Game Playing

People who play games are devoting their time and energy to unproductive tasks, so in this sense, the impact of games is obvious. Even Tim knew that team members were distracted and disengaged from the task at hand. If you want people to do something, they will do it slower and with less drive when they're enmeshed in various games.

As we noted at the beginning of the chapter, however, the impact of games is insidious. You may be able to rationalize the loss of time and energy, telling yourself that people in every group become distracted by something or don't devote 100 percent of their time to key responsibilities. The impact, though, spreads far and wide and can dramatically diminish the effectiveness of any group. To understand how this is so, consider the four main impacts of game playing:

1. *Obstacles to learning.* When games are being played frequently and intensely, managers and their direct reports often are operating from hidden agendas. They're playing for power and personal gain or to hurt someone else. They may simply enjoy the manipulation that comes with certain games. Whatever the reasons for playing them, these games foster an environment of suspicion and mistrust. Everyone is always on guard, believing that what others say isn't always what they mean.

   In this environment, it is difficult to learn and grow. Open and honest dialogue is a key to learning. When you're able to ask questions and admit that you don't know, you have a much better chance of learning something than when you rarely ask questions and have to feign competence. In game-playing environments, people are very circumspect about what they're willing to talk about, and this limits opportunities for meaningful, relationship-building dialogue. As a result, knowledge exchanges are limited. People jealously protect their knowledge, fearing that it might give someone else an advantage from an internal politics standpoint.

2. *Low morale.* Games don't just sap energy; they sap enthusiasm and interest. When people are engaged in Gotcha, Gossip, and Marginalize, they are creating cynicism on one hand and apathy on the other. When expert game players advance their careers or consolidate their power through their moves, they send the dispiriting message that games are what count in the organization, fostering an unwillingness to do anything more than what is asked. People become resigned to rampant game playing and lose interest and involvement in their tasks.

3. *Less willingness to innovate or take risks.* Self-protection is a dominant theme. People know that if they suggest something that runs counter to the conventional wisdom or that requires a departure from corporate norms, they are opening themselves up to criticism. Game-rich environments are ones where people are always looking for an edge, for a way to make themselves winners and others losers. As a result, anyone who suggests an initiative that fails or recommends a risky project that doesn't pay off becomes vulnerable.

Just as significant, people who play games often lack the motivation to be innovative. They are so focused on covering themselves in the Copy game, for instance, that they have little interest in investing the time and effort necessary to come up with truly creative concepts.

4.   *Rigidity in the face of change.* Many managers become frustrated with their people's inability or unwillingness to accept change. What these managers often don't realize is the source of this resistance. People who are actively involved in various games don't want change initiatives to be implemented, as these initiatives often make it more difficult for them to play their usual games. Change repositions people, policies, and processes, and it's difficult to play the same games with different individuals or with different ground rules in place.

Be aware, too, that this particular game impact may not be visible on the surface. People may seem to embrace change; they may say they believe that a new initiative is valuable and say they will do everything possible to make it succeed. Beneath the surface, though, their attitudes and behaviors remain the same. They resist doing anything differently and may secretly sabotage the change initiative. In fact, these covert actions against change become a new type of game, which we'll look at in Chapter Nine.

Games—a Dirty Little Corporate Secret

While interviewing for this book, we met one former CEO who admitted that his former company was rife with games, but he refused to comment on this issue if he and his company were to be identified; he thought this was an area best kept secret. It occurred to us that he and some of the managers we interviewed perceived games in the same way that adults of an earlier era viewed discussions of sex—as a conversation topic that wasn't fit for mixed company.

The impact of games is a dirty little corporate secret. At least some organizational leaders are loathe to admit that people invest a significant amount of time in these manipulative, egotistical, and hurtful behaviors. They don't want to admit that everything from their strategic planning to their hiring policies are potentially tainted by games.

Other business leaders we interviewed were willing to admit that games had some negative repercussions, but they were quick to point out that trying to do anything about their impact was futile; in their view, games functioned as a "survival of the fittest" tool. The head of a global company's business unit told us, "It's almost impossible to survive in this organization without learning how to play the games."

Another interesting phenomenon was that although people were very quickly able to describe games that took place, they rarely admitted to playing a game themselves.

What is particularly intriguing is that very few of the people with whom we talked identified games as the source of or contributors to major problems in their organizations. When things went wrong, they were quick to blame people (not enough talent), structures (need to reorganize), and strategy (have to go in a new direction). These aren't necessarily scapegoats—the problems in each area may be real—but the problems may also be fixable without hiring new talent, reorganizing, or creating a new strategy. Excessive game playing can turn A players into C players, weaken otherwise viable structures, and hamper the execution of sound strategies.

Finally, people are often reluctant to admit the impact of games because their personal identity is bound up in them. On the surface, the games we've identified come across as self-serving and time wasting, but within a cultural context, they may feel essential. Some people perceive the Gray Zone game as the ticket to their survival; it helps them avoid taking responsibility for projects they feel are doomed. The Keep Them Guessing game may feel integral to an individual's managerial style; a leader believes that by keeping his people a bit off balance, he fosters creative tension. Consequently, many professionals are reluctant to acknowledge that these games may negatively affect their effectiveness, because to do so threatens who they are at work.

Effect on Specific Leadership Functions and Tasks

Earlier we addressed the four main effects of games on organizations; here we focus on more specific, task-oriented impacts. What shocks many business leaders is that these games diminish the effectiveness of people as they go about their daily tasks. Everything from hiring decisions to execution to budgeting can be impacted negatively. And one general impact of a higher frequency of game playing is that the organization is focused inwardly (on internal games) instead of externally (on the customers, marketplace, and the external competition).

In the next sections, we examine the impact games can have on the key components of running a business listed on the following page. (Some of the games mentioned are described in the Appendix rather than in Chapter One.)

- Strategic planning
- Decision making
- Budgeting
- Setting objectives and measuring and rewarding performance
- Leading people
- Driving change

Strategic Planning

One of the primary roles of a leader is to formulate strategy. In order to do this, there are two primary requirements: a realistic assessment both of the marketplace and of the capabilities of the firm; and the formation of different and creative strategic options, followed by decision making as to which option(s) to choose.

The following are some of the key games that significantly interfere with the realistic assessment of the marketplace and the capabilities of the firm:

- *No Bad News.* Because this game entails the presentation of overly optimistic communiqués, it creates poor information flow with regard to the realities of the external or internal world.
- *The Boss Said.* Information on the marketplace or the company can be suppressed because it doesn't fit with one person's interpretation of what the CEO or senior management believes to be the case.
- *Marginalize.* Valuable information held by individuals or groups that have been marginalized does not find its way to the people who need it.

- *Big Splash Career Hopper.* Because of the desire of an individual to create a big splash, opportunities are oversold, or the current situation is made out to be worse than it is so that a bold new adventure can be launched.

Decision Making

Games subvert the decision-making process, creating environments that aren't level playing fields. Rather than allowing the right decision to be made based on the data and analysis, subjective factors enter via the following games:

- *Old War Hero.* In this game, a person who has "seen it all" downplays all new ideas by emphasizing that they have been tried before (and had failed) and expresses certainty about negative outcomes for every possible decision. This significantly interferes with the ability of the group to come up with fresh ideas and to reach consensus on a course of action.
- *Realist.* By presenting ideas as "realistic" and either explicitly or implicitly conveying that other ideas are "unrealistic," an individual creates an irrational fear of choosing any other idea than his. This can cause paralysis and prevent good discussions that would yield a better decision.
- *Excess Preparation.* An individual coerces a top team into a strategy simply by overwhelming them with the size and detail of her presentation so that the team eventually just capitulates rather than makes a thoughtful recommendation based on the facts.
- *Great Idea.* Favoritism results in the boss's overpraising one direct report's idea, creating unjustified momentum

around that idea. In this situation, the game results in the overpraised idea being adopted prematurely; other good ideas either are not suggested or are dismissed.

- *Token Involvement.* The CEO or another senior executive has already made his decision, and a meeting is held ostensibly to make the decision, but it's really all for show. If this game is played consistently, people become cynical about the decision-making process and don't contribute ideas or voice their real opinions.
- *Either-Or.* This game makes it seem as if a group were facing a black-or-white situation; you can either choose A or B, and no other possibilities exist. Even more disturbing, a manager sets up this situation by presenting one alternative in overly optimistic terms and the other in overly pessimistic ones. Thus this game limits choices and unfairly biases the choices available.

Budgeting

Budgeting is one of the key ways that organizations keep score, and the formulation of a P&L or budget is one of the areas prone to significant game playing. In their book *Beyond Budgeting*, Hope and Fraser (2003) have the following to say: "one major study of over four hundred US companies in 1987 found that budget games and manipulation were widespread, noting that 'Deferring a needed expenditure' [was the budget game] used with the greatest frequency. . . . Almost all respondents state that they engage in one or more of the budget games."

The key games in this area and their potential negative impacts are as follows:

- *The Boss Said.* When "this is what the boss wanted" is an explanation for anything that doesn't make sense, the budget suffers. This game prevents questions from being resolved and thwarts rational debate and negotiation; it also makes people cynical about budget planning because invoking the boss's name is a substitute for intelligent analysis.

- *Keep Them Guessing.* During the budget process, changes occur without logical reasons. No one is sure of the right thing to do, and short deadlines and massive amounts of paperwork add to the uncertainty. In the face of this uncertainty, people end up making budget recommendations that they think might please management, rather than ones that their business dictates.

- *Sandbagging.* The cumulative effect of this game is the setting of unambitious targets for the company, thereby losing ground to the competition and also underperforming in the stock market because of the less impressive growth curve.

- *Pecking Order.* Another game in which favorites are played; particular individuals or departments are given much more budget "relief" than other groups, undermining confidence in the whole performance management process.

- *Slush Fund.* Multiple departments secretly maintain special parts of the budget, which means that company resources aren't optimized and investment opportunities are missed.

- *Pseudo Science.* In this game, people rely on "magical ratios" or "historical precedents" to justify the size of departments or the need for certain spending patterns. They invoke noncomparable models to justify their numbers, making it impossible to engage in rational discussions about the budget.

- *Channel Stuffing.* Creating sales by stuffing the distribution channels with product and recording the result can be good for short-term fulfillment of budgets (and payment of bonuses), but distorts the picture for planning the next year's budget.

- *World on My Shoulders.* In this game, a department artificially exaggerates the huge effort its people have made to control spending or drive results, creating a better image and negotiating position for the budget cycle—often taking credit for other departments' work in the process. As a result, fat may not be trimmed from budgets because no one wants to put any more pressure on these game players than they seem to bear already.

Setting Objectives and Measuring and Rewarding Performance

A key role for any leader is to manage the performance of her people and units. But a number of games distort the ability to do this in an objective way:

- *Gotcha.* This game distorts information about performance: one small miss is amplified; also, the person who plays Gotcha seems artificially to be more deserving of recognition.

- *Gossip.* Because of the subtle, backhanded undermining of a person that goes on, the rumor mill eventually contributes to an overall impression that a particular person has not performed as well as she in fact has.

This can also happen in reverse, whereby positive gossip is used to artificially "inflate" a person's performance.

- *Blame.* This game can affect performance management in a couple of ways. The HR department can always be blamed for the unsatisfactory size of the rewards for performance (because of its policies, for instance). Blaming someone can also directly affect incentive payouts.

- *No Bad News.* This game interferes with the planning of rewards, and when the bad news finally breaks, it can seriously affect the performance management of the company or unit of the company.

- *Marginalize.* Because people have been left out of crucial discussions, it becomes much harder for them to perform, as they are missing information or data or have been moved out of the decision-making circle where they belong.

- *No Bad Feedback.* This game, by suppressing appropriate negative feedback during the year, creates a schism between perceived achievement and actual reward. It also prevents the person from adjusting and having the opportunity to improve—all for the sake of enabling the manager in avoiding the unpleasant feelings of delivering the negative feedback (actually just delaying it).

- *Entitlement.* This game engenders a feeling of immunity because of long service or friendship with a senior manager in the past, resulting in tension when rewards are passed out.

- *Management Only by Objectives.* The manager does not take into account any other factors in assessing performance (such as major uncontrollable external events, or a change of plans midyear), and this creates a climate where people feel very much hostages to fortune, or where people compete unfairly to win at all costs. This game is particularly insidious because it operates behind a guise of objectivity; it allows players to justify their decisions about promotions, bonuses, and salary increases as "perfectly logical" when those decisions are only logical from a very narrow perspective.

Leading People

Managers have to hire, deploy, motivate, and move people within the organization, and in the process of leading people, there are a whole host of games that can interfere with these objectives:

- *Gotcha, Copy, Blame, Marginalize, Great Idea, No Decision, Pecking Order, Nepotism.* These are all games that have a negative impact on the work climate, undermining team spirit, self-confidence, relationships, and sense of fair play; they may also be a cause of employee turnover.
- *Central Approval.* This game is one that leaders play to strengthen the hierarchy and bureaucracy. It disempowers everyone under a certain level who feels he must "ask permission" before doing anything. Even worse, people know what types of programs and projects are likely to get central approval, so they don't even propose anything that might be a bit risky or cutting edge. For instance, this game is often played with headcount or travel approvals.

Driving Change

Leaders must be able to drive change in their organizations so that they can adapt to changes in the external world and

maintain competitive edge, and the following games interfere with these goals:

- *Gray Zone.* Because of deliberate organizational ambiguity, the desired change is very unclear, work assignments are unclear, and territorial disputes get in the
  way of making change happen.
- *No Decision.* Delaying critical decisions about new roles
  and responsibilities can severely impact the ability of
  organizations to change.
- *Let's Not Rock the Boat.* This game can lead to conserva-
  tism in a change program or to backtracking at some
  point in the change process.
- *Hands Off.* Because of the aura of invulnerability that
  particular people or segments of the organization have
  managed to acquire, their status and roles are not properly challenged during a change effort.
- *Vague Big Vision.* This game often involves an eloquent
  articulation of a great future for the company, but it
  lacks substance. The game is to be so inspiring that a
  buzz is created around the visionary idea—a buzz that
  distorts what is possible and practical and often results
  in spending a lot of money and effort on a program
  that was doomed from the start.
- *Big Splash Career Hopper.* The organization attempts to
  implement a much too radical new design (with a lot
  of internal marketing and brochures, and usually with
  high-powered consultants) without the design's having really been thought through and without involving
  those at the grassroots level who know some of the im-
  plications of this change. This results in big problems
  at the implementation stage.

Self-Assessment

Whether you're managing a small team or a large division, the way you talk about the impact of games may be different from another manager in your organization. You may describe a "sluggishness" to your team; another manager may talk about a sense of distrust among team members. Both impacts can be the result of the same game or a combination of games. The key is to be alert to the many possible ways in which games may affect your group.

To assess the impact of games in your unit or organization, think in both internal and external terms. Monitor your own reactions to what's taking place in your group. You may feel more uncomfortable in group meetings than you did in the past; you may find that you're hesitant to be as direct and honest as you were in the past. Ask yourself too what you observe in others—your people may seem more reluctant to speak their minds or are complaining a lot.

Obviously, factors other than games can be causing these internal and external responses. Still, we've found that paying attention to games can alert you that they are having an impact on your group, especially if you find that a number of internal and external reactions are taking place. Consider the following externally oriented questions:

Is there a lot of activity taking place in your group, but with little or no progress? Do you have a lot of action plans and surface commitment to projects, but also a lack of productivity?

Have you recently launched a change initiative, but haven't achieved the expected results?

Is the group recycling the same old ideas and approaches?

Are certain topics taboo? Is it difficult to bring up certain subjects without creating a lot of tension? Do your people shy away from talking about certain issues or saying what they really believe?

Has your group's operation become overly complex or bureaucratized? Do people have to execute a lot of end runs around procedures to get something done?

Do your people frequently behave like children? Do they whine and complain about "unfairness"?

Do people act as if they don't trust each other or the organization?

Is morale low even when the company is doing well?

In thinking about these questions, recognize that pervasive game playing gums up the works: it slows things down, causes people to go through the motions, causes team members to be secretive and suspicious, and makes people feel like victims. When your direct reports are devoting their energy to games, they are distracted and distanced. Many times, managers look at their teams and understand that something is wrong but can't put their finger on what. The "what" is often games.

Now ask yourself these internally oriented questions:

Despite all my efforts as a manager, am I struggling to achieve successful results for my unit? Am I working extremely hard but not getting much accomplished?

Am I losing my drive, having to drag myself into work each morning?

Am I afraid to be direct and to confront people who aren't performing?

Do I feel I need to ask for permission before taking action?

Am I less comfortable taking risks than I was in the past?

Do I find myself becoming cynical about making changes, telling myself that they probably won't stick, so why bother?

Am I lapsing into just doing what is asked rather than going the extra mile?

Do I often fear that I am going to be punished in some way for my decisions or behaviors?

Do I believe that I am entitled to special treatment but that I'm treated unfairly?

Am I banking on a new leader coming in to save me and my group?

Games can interfere with the core processes of running a business. Therefore, they must be addressed rather than tolerated. In the next two chapters, we'll look at why such a high level of tolerance exists for games despite their destructive impact.

CHAPTER 3

Fertile Ground
Why Games Are So Pervasive in Modern Corporations

As long as organizations have existed, people have played games. Reading about the machinations of the Roman Senate thousands of years ago or the Italian princely courts at the time of Machiavelli, we can see that people have engaged in games for hundreds and even thousands of years. Human beings have devoted considerable time and energy to games throughout history.

This makes perfect sense when you realize that games are a reflexive response to anxiety. Today, they help employees deal with the anxieties of organizational life. Games serve a purpose: they are a coping mechanism (at other people's or the organization's expense) that enables people to function in challenging settings. Games are thus more prevalent when anxiety is up or when the ability to deal effectively with anxiety is down.

Although games have always been part of the organizational landscape, they are more widespread today. We live and work in an age of anxiety, volatility, uncertainty, and ambiguity. As we'll see, all these factors can drive people toward games. Reflect on your own experiences. Think about the times when your group has been concerned about its fate—after a merger or a leadership change, for instance. Maybe there was a time when a rumor of downsizing ran through the company. The odds are that during these times, you and your people played more games more intensely. Remember that in general, games are unconscious strategies people adopt to try to improve the outcomes for themselves in these times of stress; they allow people to strengthen their position within the group and weaken the positions of others; they offer a way to escape responsibility while accruing privileges.

We want to communicate the "why" behind games from macro and micro perspectives. Taking the larger view, we will describe the forces that affect organizations and create environments conducive to game playing. As we do this, be aware of how this impact translates to a smaller group setting. If you're the manager of a team of ten, you must watch for specific events and actions that can increase game-playing activity.

Let's start by examining some of the defining traits of our current era and the impact they have on games at work.

Coping Mechanism: A Response to Uncertainty

Many people work under significant amounts of stress. It is not uncommon for an individual to have a stretch assignment, to worry about job security because of a rumored downsizing, or to struggle with team members who represent different functions or who are from different countries. We're not suggesting that the current environment is all doom and gloom; stretch assignments and cross-cultural challenges are interesting as well as stressful. Our point, though, is that when the pressure is on, people resort more frequently to games. That's because games satisfy five work needs that have become increasingly compelling in recent years:

1. *The need for protection.* Games can be used as shields. The Sandbagging game, for example, provides a manager with a comfortable margin, increasing the odds that he'll be able to deliver the numbers he promises. The Copy game offers protection when a manager has a new boss, and she routinely copies this new boss on every communication she sends out in order to demonstrate her transparency and eagerness to keep the new boss in the loop. When people are under intense pressure for results, such a game seems vital for survival. When every boss is pushing every direct report for improved performance, games offer a way to deliver the appearance of results.

2. *The need for control.* If you read corporate chat boards or listen in on conversations, you'll hear employees asking these kinds of questions: "Am I in or am I out?" "Who is in control here?" and "Where are we going?" Matrix structures in an atmosphere of job insecurity contribute to fears that no one is really in charge or knows where the company is headed. This situation is scary, and people often respond to it by attempting

to find some control over their environment through games. Managers who play the Keep Them Guessing game, for instance, cause everyone in their group to be uncertain, but they make themselves feel powerful and in control because they appear to be the only ones who know the answers (and they're not telling). Similarly, people play the Blame game in order to assign specific causes to their problems. Johann blames the company's marketing people for failing to promote the product his group developed. Maria blames her boss (to other people) for killing what she felt was a breakthrough idea, without ever confronting him. Johann and Maria may know deep inside themselves that no one is really to blame—or that bad timing or the economy or bad luck is the real culprit—but they feel as if they have more control over the situation when they can assign blame to a specific person.

3. *The need for individual survival.* Pressure for short-term results often causes employees to focus more on their personal survival at the expense of the team. When they believe that it's "either he or I"—that as the pressure intensifies, some will be retained and some will be let go—they start playing games that put down their colleagues. Gotcha and Gossip are two examples of such games, allowing people to pinpoint other individuals' mistakes as well as tar their reputations. In their own minds, people may not believe that they're playing these games in order to survive; they may rationalize that the games are a way to point out mistakes in a constructive manner or to identify team members who aren't pulling their weight. The end result of the game, however,

is that there are winners and losers, and by spreading gossip and "getting" the other person, the hardest players are the winners; at least in the short term.

4. *The need for attention.* Many employees talk about feeling lost in the current organizational environment. In a matrix structure, reporting lines aren't clear, and people may believe that their voices aren't being heard. Their bosses may depart, leaving them temporarily adrift, or rotate through very quickly, which means employees need to make a good impression in a short period of time. Colleagues with whom they are closest may also leave. In these situations, people often want to broadcast their presence, and games give them a way of doing so. As children, we play games to attract adult attention and demonstrate our prowess, and the same game-playing response exists as adults. The Boss Said game quickly attracts attention, because when people mention the boss, everyone listens. Managers, too, sometimes feel as if they are being ignored, and as a result they play games that get people talking about them. When they play the No Decision game, they encourage everyone in their group to talk about the direction, the required decision, and them and what they really want. The Big Splash Career Hopper game helps a manager become the center of a new idea or massive change and enables her to point out to both her bosses and direct reports that she's critical to the organization.

5. *The need for diversion.* Both managers and their direct reports feel the pressure of trying to do more with less in lean organizations. The tight deadlines, stretch assignments, and need to learn new skills and procedures

can create a great deal of tension. Games offer the possibility of escape. Gossip is probably the most obvious escapist activity, but just about every game on our list has a smug element. We've known managers who congratulated themselves for finding clever ways to avoid making decisions. We know Gray Zone players who relish creating ambiguity and uncertainty. These games distract people from the pressures they constantly face. Although relieving that pressure is good, wasting time and valuable resources is not.

Internal and External Factors Foster Game Playing

A number of factors promote a game-playing environment.

Intense Pressure for Short-Term Performance

In the current business climate, no one wants to look as if he's not outperforming his previous quarter. Realistically, this isn't always possible. Therefore, people resort to game playing to hide or excuse or "re-baseline" their less than stellar results.

Sarbanes-Oxley and Other Rules and Regulations

New paperwork requirements, increased scrutiny on such issues as diversity, and other regulations can cause people to play games—ironically, since the legislation was intended to prevent game playing. Many times, however, people find it impossible to adhere to all the rules, and instead games emerge that allow individuals to cope with the demands—at the expense of exposing others.

The Virtual Environment

By their very nature, electronic communications are conducive to game playing. Virtual team meetings, e-mails, corporate community chat boards—all are depersonalized forms of communication that allow people to get a payoff from games without seeing firsthand the negative impact on other people. You can "say" things online that you might not ordinarily say when people are present (similar to using remote weapons in war).

Games flourish when lower levels of trust exist, and as we do more and more business virtually, this lack of person-to-person interaction breeds distrust. In this environment of distrust and increased electronic and telephone communication, games can multiply.

The Copy game is one of the most tempting games to play via e-mail, given the ease of sending e-mail copies to multiple people. The cc and bcc features make the Copy game more interesting and dangerous, and it's also possible to send an e-mail to one person and copy another person with a snide or suggestive comment about the original e-mail. Serial e-mailing can build from the communication of a simple message into a complex game. For instance, you may send Hannah an e-mail asking her to finish a project by Friday. Hannah e-mails you that she can't finish by Friday because Jonas, a manager from another function, has asked her to participate in his cross-functional team starting this week. You then send your boss a copy of Hannah's e-mail without editorial comment, knowing that this is going to push your boss's button because he's fed up with the way cross-functional teams play havoc with the schedules of various functional groups. Your boss will then e-mail Jonas protesting Hannah's participation.

E-mails also facilitate the playing of the Boss Said. Just copying the boss and noting what the boss said in a meeting to a third person can serve as a subtle virtual prod in someone's side. No Decision is another game that flourishes in a virtual environment. Because of the evanescent quality of the medium, virtual communication allows people to create the illusion that they're working hard, studying a problem, weighing alternatives, researching the issue, and studying the data. Because of the steady stream of e-mails and virtual meetings, it appears as if a lot of work is getting done. But the lack of accountability inherent in electronic communication—the absence of an individual in the room who calls for a vote to be taken—allows decisions to be postponed indefinitely.

Managers can play Token Involvement through electronic team communication to demonstrate that they really want everyone to be more involved in the decision-making process (while their actions contradict this message). Direct reports can use e-mails to suggest that a colleague is to blame for a failure.

Perhaps in the future, games won't be as ubiquitous online as they are now. As increased use of video restores more face-to-face communication, enabling people to build trust online, the temptation to play games may diminish. Now, however, the virtual world is a breeding ground for games.

Organizational Climate

We're seeing many companies where there's a growing disconnect between senior management and the rest of the company. Many senior leaders have become so busy and travel so much that they lack the time to manage by walking around. As a result of this disconnect, many employees feel insecure. They lack a sense of inclusion; they often feel that they are not being told the whole truth by management and that their ideas aren't being listened to.

Games create a false sense of inclusion, as one can perceive from the expression "He's a player." They allow people to feel part of something, even if it's part of only a superficial activity. For game players, though, this activity can generate a lot of buzz. The Gossip, Blame, and Token Involvement games, for example, are tremendously engaging. They create the impression among players that they are participating in something important and meaningful. Debating what the boss really wants can feel monumental to employees whose jobs and careers are tied to the boss's decisions. Finding someone to blame for a failure can create solidarity among those who by blaming communicate that "it wasn't my fault." When people play the Gossip game, they feel like insiders, passing on information to which only a select circle is privy. For employees who normally feel excluded and ignored, these games feel important—more important at times than their daily work.

Distrust

More so than ever before, employees are distrustful of top management. Because of well-publicized corporate scandals involving CEOs as well as equally well-publicized accounts of CEO compensation and golden parachutes, people are skeptical with regard to what their leaders have to say. They can easily hear with cynicism the CEO's pronouncements about vision and values, knowing that the CEO makes $7 million annually and is set for life, even if the company gets sold and loses value, and that he has downsized in the past and will do so in the future to make sure his numbers look good. The CEO may talk about how "we're all in this together," but many people no longer believe him.

In a distrustful atmosphere, games can gain a foothold. It's not that they allow people to trust in something else, but that they are outlets for cynicism, complaining, and manipulation. The thinking goes something like this: If I can't trust my CEO (or some other authority figure), why should I behave myself? Manipulating others you don't like through the Gray Zone or Window Watcher games feels justified. If the people at the top play games, then the people below them will follow suit. Playing games often brings out the worst in people, and the payback they get is knowing that they're not naively trusting; they feel streetwise and savvy about the way things "really work" at the company.

Organizational Flattening

Many organizations have restructured with an eye to being more flexible and innovative, adopting matrix management and launching numerous team-based initiatives. The problem is that although these flattened structures provide people with more creative freedom and push decision making down to lower levels, they also create a great deal of uncertainty. People are never quite sure to whom they report or to whom they should go with an idea or a request for resources. Are they better off dealing with their functional head or the head of their business unit or the person in charge of the office in the country where they work?

Games are a reflex response when people aren't certain of their roles and responsibilities. Games fill a vacuum—a vacuum created when the defining elements of a workplace become fuzzy. These will be a different set of games than the ones that come to the fore when organizational structures are more vertical, and authority is more certain. Without the organizational order and logic of simple structures, employees tend to create order through the games they play. In games, people have roles and goals—unproductive roles and goals, but ones that still offer people the satisfaction of doing certain tasks to achieve an end. To an outside observer, it may not seem particularly satisfying to engage in obfuscation in order to confuse your direct reports and keep them on their toes, but in those moments when you're playing this game, doing so meets a need, even if only in reinforcing your reports' dependence on you.

Hierarchical Structures

Games flourish in environments where positional power prevails and great gaps exist between the haves and have-nots. We see these gaps widening when top executives reward themselves with perks, and accrue more control while others are being asked to do more with less and are in constant danger of being downsized. In these environments, games can become part of an individual leader's character and by extension a characteristic of the entire organization.

People at the bottom of the pyramid often feel powerless and depersonalized, which make them turn to games for a number of reasons.

First, they feel that management doesn't take them seriously and views them as inconsequential. When they're treated like children, they act like children. Thus such games as Sandbagging and Victim have great appeal.

Second, they resort to games to achieve certain work goals. Because they've been depersonalized and disempowered, they feel they can't get things done through regular channels. Games form an alternative route to getting what they want. They may believe that they must "tar" a colleague in order to move him out of the way and get his job (Marginalize). They may be convinced that the only way they can keep their job is by hiding any bad news from their boss (No Bad News). Or they may need to hire a consultant to justify some of their leadership decisions (Scapegoat). So they devote their energies to these games and accomplish certain objectives (at a cost to their companies).

Third, some employees react to depersonalizing hierarchical structures by becoming angry. They are like closet revolutionaries, plotting anarchy. In these instances, people can use games to sabotage team or group efforts. They can spread rumors through games that create counterproductive conflict. They can use games to waste time and effort and lower morale, draining a team of its energy and cohesiveness.

Having said all of this, it is easy to play the Blame game with senior management. Often employees are apathetic and all too happy to cede authority up the organization in exchange for the right to play the Victim.

Performance Management and Categorization

One last organizational trend promotes games: categorizing employees in terms of their performance. People are known as A, B, or C players and high-potentials. They receive exacting performance reviews. They are seen as leaders. They are asked to acquire the competencies of a leadership profile. We're not saying that categorizing employees is all bad, but doing so in a way that is strongly tied to personal consequences places a great deal of pressure on people who are categorized favorably, and it makes those who are categorized as C players or "contributors" feel disenfranchised. In both cases, games seem like a viable option. Employees labeled as high-potentials use games to reinforce their position (for example, by playing such games as Lowballed Baseline, Kill the Messenger, or Big Splash Career Hopper). Employees labeled as C players use games cynically or for the purpose of sabotage (for example, by playing Victim, Gossip, or No Decision).

Portrait of a Game-Playing Team

Terrence is a forty-one-year-old manager with a large, traditional manufacturing organization—at least it used to be traditional. For years, the company was one of the stellar performers in the industry, regularly turning a profit and growing at a strong pace. Around 2001, the company was hit hard on a number of fronts—global competitors eroded share, its manufacturing technology needed a major overhaul, it was facing an Environmental Protection Agency investigation about its chemical disposal policies, and it had received negative publicity about the small number of women and minorities in executive ranks and was defending itself against a discrimination lawsuit. During this time, Terrence's boss and his boss's boss departed, and Terrence was reassigned to head a new group with only two of his former direct reports—the rest were either new hires or transfers from other groups.

The new CEO had warned everyone that the changes he had made weren't the last, and the implicit threat was that no one's job was secure unless the company made a significant turnaround. To help achieve this turnaround, everyone was working longer and harder than ever before. A number of new policies, processes, and programs had been instituted to improve productivity, including a new software system with which Terrence and his group were struggling. In addition, Terrence was one of many managers being asked to attend special executive development training, designed to help them learn the new CEO's approach and become more proactive and flexible in their management style.

Terrence felt overwhelmed, as did his direct reports, and it had a significant impact on his managerial style. Previously, Terrence had always been clear in his assignments. He took pride in his ability to communicate with his people and help them complete their tasks. Now, though, Terrence was confused, in part because during the executive development program, the trainer had advocated adopting a looser, more ambiguous style to catalyze creativity among direct reports. Terrence was also anxious about his job and had started putting out feelers to see if there were openings at another organization.

As a result, he started playing Gray Zone and No Decision. He didn't do so consciously, but he thought that if he didn't define tasks clearly and left it to his direct reports to determine who should do what to accomplish objectives, he would foster a more innovative mind-set among his group. Terrence also was distracted from the tasks at hand, worried about his future with the company and a possible job at another company. He was now afraid of making any decision that could affect his image and career. He was not in the mood to cross his *t*'s and dot his *i*'s. For the first time in his career, Terrence was not being diligent and efficient, allowing his own uncertainty to creep into his management approach.

Terrence was meeting his needs for protection and survival, and, by playing those games, his payoff was a false feeling of security that helped him cope with the uncertainty of the environment—at a cost to his direct reports and his team's performance.

Assess the Impact of Trends and Events on Your Group's Games

Within the past year or so, certain developments within and outside your organization may have increased the propensity of you and your people to play games, as they did in Terrence's situation. Although it's impossible to know definitively how each event affected each individual in your group, you can make a good guess about the general impact on game playing. To help you make this guess, we've created a series of questions that will allow you to broadly assess how your environment may be set up for games at work:

Have your people come under increased pressure for results in recent months? Are deadlines tighter, stretch assignments more common, work hours longer, and group goals more ambitious?

Has the organizational tolerance for failure decreased? Are there more serious consequences if your group doesn't meet stated objectives?

Has your organization undergone a significant change in the past year—a downsizing, merger, or acquisition?

Has this change resulted in high turnover at the leadership level?

Are managers in your organization expected to be superheroes? Are they required to do more in less time than ever before? Are they given a wider range of responsibilities than in the past?

Is your organization very hierarchical, with people at the bottom feeling disempowered?

Has your organization become increasingly inclined to categorize people in terms of A, B, or C players or high-potentials? Are there serious personal consequences depending on the category? Do people who aren't favorably categorized feel disgruntled or disenfranchised?

Compared to a year or two earlier, is there a widening gap between your people and management? Do your people complain of being disrespected or treated unfairly?

Has your company experienced any scandal or ethically questionable behavior on the part of management (golden parachutes, discrimination lawsuits, executive privilege gone overboard) that have alienated people? Have they responded to these events with cynicism, mistrust, or feelings of victimization?

Have you moved toward a more virtual workplace? Are you using more phone conferences, virtual teams, and other electronic communication in place of face-to-face interactions?

Has your organization recently been restructured, moving to a complex matrix structure? Are reporting lines less clear than in the past? Are people confused about what the organization expects of them and how their performance is measured?

Has morale within your organization or your team gone down recently? Is it because of permanent changes at the top of the organization, such as a new CEO or new policies and procedures? Is it a result of people's generally feeling less secure about their jobs?

If you answered yes to at least a few of these questions, it's quite possible that the conditions in your organization are hospitable to games. Of course, the organizational environment and your group's environment can be different. You may have taken steps to reduce the influence of negative external and internal events on your people; consciously or not, you may have made it less likely that these developments caused your people to be more avid game players. Consider the following questions relative to your own actions as a manager:

Have you attempted to channel productively any anxiety created by an atmosphere of instability and insecurity within your team, without false promises?

Have you done everything possible to be transparent about your actions, even if transparency isn't a quality other leaders exhibit?

When a negative event has an impact on your company and creates low morale, fear, stress, and so on, do you make an effort to engage in dialogue with your people about this event? Do you encourage them to ask questions, and respond with as much information as you can?

Do you make an effort to facilitate face-to-face meetings and other personal interactions to supplement virtual communication? Do you eschew e-mail at times for one-on-one talks with your people?

Do you help your people deal with the stress that they're under? Do you encourage them to tell you when they're feeling overwhelmed? Do you offer practical ideas and your own involvement to reduce their stress at times? Do you talk to your own boss to get your people help when you believe that they are being asked to do too much?

Have the increased stress, pressure for short-term results, virtual communication, and other factors caused you to play games yourself? Thinking back on your behaviors with your team, have you started playing some of the games listed in Chapter One?

Have you assigned equal importance to short-term results and long-term objectives, to creating profit and to growing people—by, for example, instituting a balanced scorecard approach?

Have you made a consistent effort to keep politics out of daily corporate life and create an atmosphere of trust and respect?

If you determine that you haven't done much to prevent your people from responding to the environment with game playing, recognize that you're not alone. The internal and external forces we've been describing are powerful. Managers and leaders are as likely to be drawn into a game-playing ge-stalt as anyone else. If you work in an organization that has become highly politicized, for example, people are naturally going to play games in order to curry favor with the right people or hurt those who threaten their positions.

Unfortunately, in today's climate, responding "yes" to the majority of the preceding questions isn't always realistic. Let's look at why this is so.

CHAPTER 4

Eyes Wide Shut
Why People Don't Deal with Games at Work

W hy don't organizations clamp down on games? More specifically, why don't individual managers stop the game playing in their groups? Even more specifically, why don't individuals recognize that playing these games has a harmful effect on their productivity—and potentially their learning and development—and stop them on their own?

The answers to these questions are as complex as human beings themselves. As you've learned, people play games for many reasons, including reasons of individual psychology and personal history. In organizational settings, games may be part of the culture, so playing them feels right. As we've said, people frequently aren't even conscious that they're playing games.

Four Reasons Not to Confront Games

Let's look at the four most common reasons why people typically do not confront games at work.

Lack of Awareness

Gossiping doesn't feel like a game but like something that's a natural part of the workday. Gray Zone may seem like a useful tool to manage and motivate people. When you don't define a game as a game, you lack the awareness necessary to do something about it. Even if you're not playing the game yourself but you notice that your people are playing Blame against each other routinely, you chalk it up to human nature. It is easier to notice game playing in others than to notice it yourself. How can you put a stop to something that feels as natural as meetings and as integral to the workplace as e-mailing? If they notice anything, people might refer to what they see around them as "just politics" or "human nature."

In addition, up until now there has been no language to describe game playing in organizations; it is difficult to be aware of something for which you have no language. We hope that this book will bring the necessary language to the workplace and help fill that gap.

Payoffs

Many people engage deliberately in game playing (although they would call it "the end justifying the means" rather than describe themselves as playing games) either to look good or to avoid looking bad. People in this category might use such phrases as "If you are not inside, you are outside" (popularized by the movie *Wall Street*). The Lowballed Baseline game certainly helps many managers appear to be performing better than they actually are.

In *Human Motivation,* David McClelland (1988) advances what is sometimes known as the *three needs theory.* He suggests that people over the course of their lives develop needs that fall mainly into three categories: the need for affiliation, the need for power, and the need for achievement (to varying degrees for different people). Some of the payoffs from games build at least temporarily on one or another of these needs. Let's look at them in turn.

Affiliation

Games bind people together. Onboarding is at least in part about learning the games of an organization. In a way, it's a socialization process that allows new employees to figure out the way things work in a given culture and how they can survive and do well. Once they understand that Keep Them Guessing is an accepted and tacitly endorsed game, they can join in and feel part of something larger than themselves. In many games, people are assigned different roles—winner and loser, victim and victimizer, catalyst and responder, rescuer and workaholic—and even though not all these roles have pleasant outcomes, they confer a sense of belonging. If you have a role, you have a place in the organization.

Even managers who don't like the games that are being played want to foster a sense of inclusion. They are reluctant to curtail the rituals and activities that create camaraderie among their people. They may see accepting games as making a trade-off—wasted time and energy for teamwork.

In reality, of course, the inclusion fostered by games is fleeting and superficial. People don't experience the sense of satisfaction and collaboration that they can when they work long and hard together to seize an opportunity or solve a problem. They can create real inclusion by spending productive energy working together and succeeding.

Power

Obviously, some organizational managers have a need for power—from a modest need for influence to an obsessive need for control over other people's lives. Participation in many of the work games we've discussed helps meet this need. These people have a tendency toward megalomania, and are willing to use games to this end. Typical games might include Central Approval, Show Up Differently, No Bad News, Gotcha, Kill the Messenger, Marginalize, and other games that project and reinforce power.

Direct reports, too, may have a need for power, but they may pursue this payoff as Machiavellian advisers to the prince. For them, games of flattery and insinuation (such as Public Challenge of Your Loyalty, Half-Truth, Pampering a VIP, Deliberate Leak, and the Boss Said) allow them to experience the thrill of power without formally possessing it.

We've described some of these games in earlier chapters, but others are new to you. The need for power generates distinct games that other needs do not. To give you a sense of these power games, here are a few capsule descriptions of the games in action:

- *Central Approval.* In order to control headcount increases, Estella, the CEO of a company, creates a rule that all people replacements need to be approved by her.
- *Show Up Differently.* Hassan shows up in different meetings in different moods (angry, upset, calm, rational, impulsive, and so on) so that you never know which Hassan is going to be present. This keeps his subordinates on edge and adds to Hassan's power.
- *Public Challenge of Your Loyalty.* When Sol raises some legitimate concerns with the way the organization is

approaching an issue, Brent challenges Sol's loyalty to the organization or to the proposal, rather than responding to Sol's concerns. Brent gains power by suggesting that he has the interests of the company at heart and Sol doesn't.

People who play games for power are extremely reluctant to give up these behaviors. In extreme cases, such as certain dictators, the only way they give up the games is through assassination or a military coup. In a corporate setting, the "dictator" would be deposed through a boardroom coup, through whistle blowing, or a swift and unexpected economic collapse of the company.

Achievement

Games are ways to fulfill the items on your own agenda. The player can achieve short-term goals through games, although doing so may not be particularly worthwhile in the long run. They can prompt people to work harder and make the department or team look as if it's performing better. By definition, you can win a game, and that conveys a sense of accomplishment. If you're not deriving that sense of accomplishment from your actual work, games provide a substitute that is difficult to let go of. For example, the Lowballed Baseline game helps managers feel as if they have found a good way to meet their numbers.

When Juan copies Angelica's boss on the request for a customized report he needs in two days, he feels that he is helping achieve his objectives. Some games might not get things done quickly or effectively, but they provide "shadow" processes for doing work tasks. The No Decision game helps people avoid making mistakes, and in so doing enables them to preserve their record of mistake-free performance.

Rationalization

People tell themselves that they need to use the manipulative, win-lose behaviors of games in order to survive. They convince themselves that games are the price they pay for being a manager or for working in a highly competitive environment—and that anyone who doesn't play them will be down and out. Hundreds of rationalizations exist, allowing people to convince themselves that their behaviors make sense within an organizational context. They may studiously avoid being dishonest or manipulative in their personal lives, but they're able to rationalize these actions in a work setting. The apt phrase in this category is "You have to play the game" (one of the few phrases that hints at what is really going on in organizations).

It is this sort of rationalizing that can cause perfectly normal human beings to participate in some of the awful tragedies of the industrial era, such as the Pinto scandal. In the case of the Pinto, the unwillingness to challenge a collective game playing allegedly cost many drivers and passengers of the infamous vehicle their lives (see the case of *Grimshaw* v. *Ford Motor Co.*) because of Ford's decision to place the fuel tank in what proved to be an unsafe position in the car.

Fear

Managers and individual contributors fear withdrawing from a game or challenging others who play because they believe they may be critiqued or even ostracized—that they may become victims of the Marginalize game. They also believe that they may become targets for retaliation. These are very real fears: senior managers generally do not like the idea that in their professional organizations there are games going on; it is damaging to the image of the firm.

Suyin, a young executive who had recently joined a large professional services firm, couldn't believe how much time members of her group spent playing the Boss Said game. It seemed as if everyone's trump card during meetings was to justify their own points of view by referring to what Shubao (their division head) wanted. In one meeting, Suyin became fed up with this behavior and asked why everyone always felt compelled to mention Shubao's name when they were stating their own opinions. Immediately, everyone began criticizing Suyin, telling her that it was important to understand the direction that Shubao was setting, that she hadn't been there long enough to understand how perceptive Shubao was about issues, and so on. Stung by the intensity of their criticism, Suyin was afraid to bring up the subject again.

To open a metaphorical can of worms means delving into complicated issues and, through this investigation, creating problems that seemingly make matters worse than when you ignored the can. Managers fear the consequences of opening the issue of game playing to public scrutiny. They believe that it will upset the functioning of the group and possibly the organization. They envision arguments and counterarguments about the games they identify. They picture a lot of time and emotional energy wasted as an internal debate rages about how to control game playing. It strikes them that it might be better to leave well enough alone (though of course rampant game playing is not "well enough").

Some leaders, too, have provided us with another can-of-worms argument. They note that typically, people in an organization are aware of one prominent game—the Sandbagging game, for example. If they decide to challenge this game, they recognize that they're likely to fail in the attempt. Later we'll talk more about the ecology of games and how games are interconnected in corporations. Here, though, the point is that the ecology of games can form the behavioral norms of a corporate culture—if you attempt to eliminate one game, you're challenging the culture. As a result, the challenge fails. You're simply attacking one game, which just stirs people up and causes them to protest. It's akin to challenging, for example, labor communes in a communist country. If you challenge only one part of a larger system, the system will rise up and strike back. If you challenge the basis for the entire system—in our example, communism itself—then in the long run there is a higher chance of success.

Another aspect of the can-of-worms argument is that if you call a halt to game playing, you may be accused of calling the kettle black. Not to mix metaphors, but most of us are guilty of going along with or playing games at some point in our careers. Even if you've participated unwittingly—prior to your heightened awareness of the games being played—you may come across as a hypocrite if you attack them. For this reason, many leaders pause before making public statements against games. Looking back, they realize that they blamed and gossiped, copied and lowballed with the best of them.

Finally, there may also be a fear of being perceived as being negative, or even "naming names." No one wants to be perceived as a snitch. No one wants to be seen as always looking at the dark side of human behavior. People fear that if they name games and ask people to curtail their gaming, they will earn reputations that won't help them move up in the organization.

Why Aren't You Confronting Games at Work?

In going through the reasons why games aren't identified and curtailed, you may have wondered which reason applied to you or your people. Are you oblivious to games being played in your group? Are you aware of them but worried that talking about them will create more problems than you already have?

To help you answer the questions, the following are checklists of statements made by people who use the given reasons, which correspond to those we've discussed in this chapter. Go through each checklist and note which statements you might make. The list or lists in which you put the most checks are probably representative of the reasons you use to avoid managing games in your group.

Lack of Awareness
- ☐ I don't play games at work.
- ☐ I don't believe my people play games.
- ☐ A few of my direct reports may occasionally engage in manipulative, unproductive, and other negative behaviors, but I think these behaviors are natural.
- ☐ Some individuals in my group play games, but it doesn't take much of their time, and I don't see it having any negative effect.
- ☐ At work we have a lot of politics, but I wouldn't call it game playing.

Payoffs
- ☐ I am able to exert control over people through game playing.

- [ ] Work is one big game with winners and losers, so you have to learn to play the game well.
- [ ] People who don't play games in our company don't get ahead.
- [ ] Sometimes when you can't get things accomplished through straightforward actions, you need to resort to the games that are unofficially sanctioned in your company.
- [ ] Games provide important shortcuts when deadlines loom and the pressure is on.
- [ ] Without games, I would lose much of my ability to handle my team.
- [ ] To be effective, people need to be controlled and kept under stress.
- [ ] In our highly structured organization, power is crucial for leaders to be effective.
- [ ] In our company, the best game players have the most power.
- [ ] Games provide us with a way to achieve goals. Calling for an end to games will waste a lot of energy on debating the subject, making accusations, and so on.

Rationalization
- [ ] I can't manage effectively unless I use certain games.
- [ ] You have to play games in our company to protect yourself.
- [ ] Games are always going to be played, so you can either try to use them to your advantage or be victimized by them.
- [ ] Games are part of the ingrained politics of the corporation.

- [ ] I don't like manipulative behaviors and hidden agendas, but they're just part of corporate life and how things work. People are always going to be jockeying for position and power, and game playing is one of the ways this happens.
- [ ] Corporate gamesmanship is a necessary evil.
- [ ] People at the top of our company are political animals.
- [ ] Politics-based games may not be nice or particularly useful, but they come with the organizational territory. There is just too much game playing going on for one person to be able to do anything about it.

Fear

- [ ] I would be ostracized within the organization if I were to speak out against games.
- [ ] I worry that without games, my people will lose their energy and commitment.
- [ ] I don't want to be viewed as a traitor or tattletale.
- [ ] People who inform on others may receive formal commendations from management, but no one will ever trust them again.
- [ ] As bad as games are, being a whistleblower is worse.
- [ ] We function okay even with the games; better to leave well enough alone.
- [ ] In the past, I've been guilty of playing games; I don't want to raise the alarm and then be accused of being a hypocrite. I am afraid that calling an end to games will open a can of worms in our team (organization).

Bad Reasons, Good Excuses: Challenge Your Assumptions

Be aware of the particular reasons you use to allow games to be played uninterrupted and unimpeded. Recognize that although some of the reasons may have some validity, ultimately they are nothing more than excuses that harm your group's productivity and your company's profitability.

Now that you understand the downside of games and why they flourish despite the damage they cause, you're ready to do something about them. Let's look at what can be done at an individual and organizational level to try to regain some of the productivity losses caused by games.

CHAPTER 5

An Eye-Opening Experience
Awakening to Games

Why don't people wake up and stop playing counterproductive games? We've tried to answer that question earlier from an organizational perspective, explaining the common obstacles that allow games to flourish in all types of companies. But now we'd like to shift our focus to an individual perspective, because it's crucial for you to view games both individually and organizationally. Here and in the next two chapters, we want to address the three-step process you can use to emerge from a game-playing state and recognize that you have other options than to participate in or ignore the games that are being played.

The three steps of what we call the ACE method are Awakening, Choice, and Execution. Awakening is a raising of your consciousness about games and gaining awareness of the games you and others are engaged in. Once you have awakened to games, the next step is Choice: making the decision to continue playing or to stop. The third and final step,

Execution, entails putting new game-free behaviors into effect. Figure 5.1 illustrates the ACE method.

Sleeping Beauty: A Trance-Like State

A popular fairy tale tells of a princess who pricks her finger on a magic spindle and falls to sleep in her castle. She remains asleep while all around her castle, the thorns grow. It is only when a prince manages to cut through the thorns, reach Sleeping Beauty, and kiss her that she wakes up. We believe that Sleeping Beauty is an apt metaphor for many organizations, asleep while all around them the games grow, cutting the companies off from the outside world (the world of customers, markets, and competitors).

Reading this book may seem sufficient to alert you to the danger of games and get you to manage them more effectively. After all, once you've identified the games being played in your group, how difficult could it be simply to say,

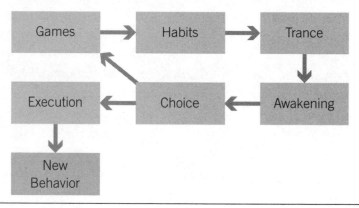

FIGURE 5.1 The ACE Method

"Here are the games we've been playing; here are the negative impacts; enough!"?

Unfortunately, games insinuate themselves into our work habits and consciousness. We don't usually notice them, just as we don't always notice that we have to tie our shoelaces every morning. If you're at an organization for any length of time, the activities that make up games become repetitive actions, segue to routines, and then settle in as reflexes. This is what we have termed reverse evolution. When games reach the reflex state, they have transformed from a conscious activity to a subconscious reaction.

Because of the viral nature of games, they can quickly spread from one person to the next. Often a game's sheer ubiquitousness renders it almost invisible. Essentially, the game turns into an organizational norm, an accepted way of dealing with certain types of people and situations. The combination of reflex and norm produces a trance-like state—a Sleeping Beauty organization. You no longer have to think about why you're playing a game or how it might have a negative effect. It has become organizationally sanctioned (the norm) and a natural way of acting (the reflex). So you (or people in your group) slip into the game as easily as you slide under the covers at night.

As we mentioned earlier in the book, you're most likely to be alert to and aware of games when you first join a company. At this point, you haven't been indoctrinated to the games played in your particular corner of the organization. They haven't yet become part of the wallpaper. Even if game playing went on at your previous employer, the odds are that a different mix of games is being played at your new company. As a result, you notice them; you're aware of their negative effects.

Let's say you become the manager at an organization where lots of game playing takes place around budgets. People play the Sandbagging game in which they lowball sales forecasts as a negotiating tactic. Or they play the Slush Fund game and purposely disguise an item that's designed to allow them to overspend. You immediately notice these and other budget-related games, and you are aghast at how much effort goes into manipulating others around budget issues through distorting, omitting, or exaggerating real information, and at how this manipulation results in money spent that isn't in line with strategic objectives. You start talking to your bosses and colleagues about this situation, and here is what you hear in response:

"This is just the way we do things around here. And it works."

"The systems are set up to accommodate working with budgets in this way."

"The CEO wants us to do it this way."

"Interesting; why don't you write up your thoughts on the subject in a white paper?"

"You're right, but don't rock the boat. Work with it for a year, and if you still feel strongly after that time, we'll talk again."

In fact, you won't talk again. After a year of working in an environment where budget games are rife, you'll become accustomed to them. What at first seemed to be odd, counterproductive behavior will feel like second nature after a while. The trance-like state will envelop you, and even if you don't join in and play the budget games, you'll accept that others are playing them.

When we refer to "trance-like," we obviously don't mean that people in a given work group interact like a bunch of zombies. The trance-like behaviors are more subtle, if not any less mind numbing. Here are some common traits of people in this state:

- They reach consensus easily and quickly, and rarely engage in productive debate or conflict (though there may well be back stabbing).
- They exhibit a concern with personal career goals and reputation to the exclusion of group goals.
- They are unresponsive when others challenge some of the key organization processes.
- They are fixated on what the boss wants (rather than focused on what they feel is the right thing to do).
- They are reluctant to consider the long-term consequences of actions.

Think about whether these traits describe how you or the people in your group typically act and interact. To help you make this determination, try the following exercise:

1. Recall the first few months following your beginning to work at your organization (or in a particular group within the organization). Think about what struck you as odd or unusual about how people in your group or other colleagues acted. Did you remark to friends or former colleagues about this behavior? Do you remember questioning your boss or work peers about it?

2. Think about what these odd or unusual behaviors revolved around. Did they have to do with budgetary

issues? Were they designed to boost one's career within the organization? Did they involve protecting oneself? Did they have to do with the openness of communication (or lack thereof)?

3. In a given group, what percentage of people displayed these particular behaviors? Was it just a few people, or was it widespread, including managers as well as direct reports? After asking these questions, determine if these behaviors weren't limited to your particular group but were instead part of the organizational DNA.

4. Has your attitude changed about these behaviors (assuming at least one year has passed since you joined the company or a particular group)? Do they no longer seem odd or counterproductive? Have you rationalized the way people act?

Warning Signs: Interpreting What Game Players in a Trance Are Really Saying

What looks like trance-like behavior to a newcomer may seem perfectly natural to someone who has been around awhile. Your group may seem to be functioning effectively, so to your eye, at least, no one appears to be sleepwalking through her job. Yet if you listen closely to the dialogue in which you and your people engage, you may discover that you're saying things that people in trances typically say. Rather than being straight with other people, communicating your vulnerabilities and resolving conflicts, you're procrastinating, blaming, and relying on organizational clichés.

Here are some examples of trance-like statements made by people who are playing games:

"I know it doesn't make sense, but would you mind doing it that way? We need it for Kenji [a senior VP]."

This is the type of statement that reflects the irrational, counterproductive mind-set of people who aren't thinking clearly. If something doesn't make sense, why do it that way? Is it really worth pleasing Kenji if the effort will waste time and money?

"Don't bring up _____ in the meeting; it's a touchy subject."

It's also probably a subject that requires debate and discussion, but people don't want to engage in this activity because they know it will wake them from their trance and force them to engage in conflict.

"Devorah [a senior executive] is not happy with you, but I told her you really did have good intentions."

Why isn't Devorah telling you this herself? And the person telling you this is clearly trying to upset you while at the same time absolving himself from fault. Indirect, agenda-laden dialogues suggest that people are not fully engaged and aware.

"You know how HR is; they told me that I couldn't give you a raise of more than ___ percent."

This statement suggests that in this company, HR creates irrational policies and people play games around them. If HR's policies really control raise levels and deserving people don't receive proper raises, then people are accepting an irrational system.

"Don't worry; the situation will resolve itself."

People in trances don't like taking decisive action. When they are talking about seeing how things will play out and allowing events to take their course, they often are avoiding rousing themselves from their torpor and making a difficult decision.

"In private, the CEO told me . . ."

If it was private, why are you sharing it? Again, this line of dialogue reflects an environment where information is communicated indirectly (if at all). People can play games like the Boss Said because in the hazy, half-awake world in which they operate, straight talk is uncommon.

Even if the games themselves have become invisible, the trance-like conversations are readily apparent. People who are fully alert and involved in the work itself don't communicate important information indirectly or accept irrational policies or avoid all conflict. These telltale dialogues are signs of game-based dysfunction, and you need to sound an alarm and wake up to the danger. Up to this point, we've suggested how you can do so intellectually. An emotional wake-up is also necessary, however, so let's examine what that entails.

Feeling Alarmed

Let's assume that you've become aware that game playing is occurring in your organization. Whether or not you're participating, you now perceive that many employees are sleepwalking through important aspects of their jobs. Yet this intellectual awareness probably won't translate into action unless there is an emotional awareness as well. It's one thing to wake up to the problem of games. It's something else to act once you've been woken.

An emotional reaction to games furnishes the energy necessary to change behaviors and break out of game routines. Don't underestimate the hold that a trance-like state has on people. It's comfortable and familiar, and for many employees, it feels like the right way to work, especially after they're acclimatized to the organization. It's only when people become sad and regretful about how much time they've wasted that they are motivated to change. Or it may be that managers become angry because they realize that they haven't treated people fairly and that they've lost people—whether to other employers or in a more figurative sense—because of their game-playing behaviors. Whatever the emotion, it serves as a motivating wake-up call. When you feel that you've lost opportunities to implement creative solutions or to grow people, your sadness, disappointment, anger, and resentment all produce energy.

This energy counteracts the energy used to play games. Consider the case of Ricardo, a marketing executive in a global company. Ricardo was smart, talented, and highly successful, promoted three times in six years. He knew not only how to deliver results but how to play the company's dominant games. He excelled at Token Involvement, in the end always dominating his people so that they would eventually reinforce his point of view. And he was great at Gotcha, riding people hard when he believed they had made a wrong decision or other type of mistake.

What's interesting is that Ricardo wasn't nitpicking or manipulative in his personal life. A loyal and compassionate father and spouse, he had strong values. But when he arrived at work, he fell under the spell of his organization's games. The ecology of games revolved around managers being "tough" with their people as well as covering themselves with their bosses. This was just the way it was, and this was how Ricardo believed leaders must behave in order to thrive within the organization.

Ricardo only started to wake up from the games-induced trance when a new CEO came in and began changing the culture—and the games that were played. She insisted that all executives above a certain level—including Ricardo—had to undergo 360-degree feedback from their teams as part of a mentoring program. The CEO was shocked to hear that many of Ricardo's direct reports felt that they were just worker bees for him, that he didn't care anything about their growth and development, that he was dictatorial and mean-spirited, and that a lot of their time was spent just trying to avoid getting on his bad side.

Through a discussion with a coach about this feedback, Ricardo recognized that he was playing certain games without consciously considering them games. Cognitively, he became aware of what those games involved. But it wasn't until Ricardo allowed his feelings about this feedback to emerge that he generated the energy necessary to behave differently. This wasn't a quick and clean process. At first, his major emotion was anger that this feedback meant he wasn't going to receive another promotion in the near future. His anger also produced denial of the feedback; he attempted to argue that the feedback was flawed because it came after some people in his division were let go, which prejudiced the results. It was a few weeks before this anger passed and Ricardo was able to come to terms with the sadness that resided beneath the anger.

What facilitated this fresh emotion was Ricardo's meeting with his team and discussing the feedback. The session was humbling, but it was also liberating in a way. It wasn't that people in Ricardo's group thought he was untalented or a bad person. Just about everyone told him that he was extremely bright and knowledgeable about the business and that they admired his ability to generate results. But they also shared their disappointment that he had acted the way he did, and how his leadership behaviors had stunted their professional growth and prevented them from taking risks that might have further bolstered results.

In the weeks following this meeting, Ricardo's sadness lingered and created the energy we referred to earlier. Although this energy clearly has an upside, it can also have a downside. Specifically, it can turn to self-aggression. In other words, a person can beat herself up for all her counterproductive game-playing activities. Ricardo, for instance, was furious at himself for being oblivious to the impact of his behaviors. He was in danger of wasting his energy on punishing himself—self-flagellation can turn into another game of sorts. Fortunately, the support of his team and a coach helped him move on to the Choice phase of the ACE process and funnel his energy in a positive direction.

What every professional needs to remember is that to play games is human. To beat yourself up over your participation in or passive acceptance of game playing is nonsensical.

Recognize that waking from your trance provides you with an opportunity to moderate the game playing in your area.

Seizing the Opportunity: Accepting and Moving Forward

How do you transform emotion into positive energy? The following steps should prove useful for you and your people:

1. When you feel sad, angry, or disappointed, or experience any other feeling upon learning about the games played, express your feelings to someone you trust. This might be a coach, your boss, a colleague—anyone with whom you feel comfortable. Expressing your feelings helps channel the energy in a positive direction rather than allowing it to turn into self-aggression.

2. Talk about your feelings in terms of specific games. Explore the particular games you or your group have engaged in and why these games were so appealing and "natural" at the time. Express how these games made you feel involved, in control, powerful, and so on. It's useful to talk about your feelings then as opposed to those you are experiencing now. For instance, perhaps you've played the No Bad News game in order to avoid getting into conflicts with your people or to prevent your boss from shooting the messenger. At the time, you felt relieved because the game allowed you to avoid the fights and anger that would come with straight talk. Now you feel regretful at having missed opportunities to grow your people or sad that you were so fearful of your boss's negative responses that you withheld

critical information from him. By talking about your game-related feelings then and now, you can place these games in an emotional context.

3. Validate your real needs. Recognize that what motivated you to play these games are real needs that require attention and that you now can find some other way to take care of them. For example, trying to avoid fights and anger might imply a legitimate need for respect for people and affiliation. Notice that you can still attend to this need without playing a game.

4. Accept and forgive your game playing. Recognize that you are human. Consider how your organizational culture made the particular games you played so accessible and approved. Recognize that no matter the damage this game playing may have done to your company or your people, you now have the opportunity to improve. Resolve to work more transparently and more creatively to deal with organizational issues, and to rely less on games to deal with them.

Let's now look at the choices with which your awakening presents you.

CHAPTER 6

Count Me Out
Choosing Not to Play

Once people awaken to the reality of games, why don't they simply choose to opt out? On the surface, it seems so simple: games waste time and energy; the manager becomes aware of games; the manager decides to stop participating in or facilitating them.

Only it's not so simple. Games meet powerful needs, whether for approval, promotion, camaraderie, or continued employment, and it may seem to participants that they can't get those needs met any other way. Therefore, even when their eyes are opened to the existence of games within their group, they do nothing. Even though they know that games are bad, the alternative seems worse.

Whether they're making a conscious or unconscious decision, the fact is that people choose to keep playing. They have alternatives to this choice, but to understand them, we first need to explore how games help diminish the anxiety most people feel in the typical stress-filled organization.

Needs, Anxiety, and Choice

Psychologist Abraham Maslow (1987) has posited that we are all born with a hierarchy of needs: physiological needs (such as the need for food and water), safety needs (such as the need for shelter), needs for love and belonging, needs for esteem, and needs for self-actualization. We spend much of our time trying to meet these needs, but when we're not sure if they are going to be met, we become anxious. According to Maslow, when a first-order need is met, we start becoming anxious about a second-order need. Further, even when we meet our current needs, we become anxious about whether we're going to be able to meet these needs in the future. That's why we try to secure a future supply chain for these needs.

In the context of a modern corporation, an employee might feel that to meet these needs she must keep a job, secure approval from a boss (informally or through a formal process, such as a performance review), and receive a promotion, bonus, or salary increase. Obviously, when a given employee questions her ability to do any or all of these things, she becomes anxious. And, as noted, people may be meeting these needs in the present but be uncertain about meeting them in the future. Perhaps a new CEO has been brought in, and the rumor is that he plans to recruit his own people for key jobs. Perhaps a competitor is making inroads, revenue is down, and it's possible that there will be a downsizing. Perhaps it's something as simple as the arrival of a new boss with whom an individual doesn't hit it off immediately.

When times are stressful or uncertain, there are a number of ways to try to allay this anxiety. Obviously, doing a good job helps, whether as an individual performer or as a manager. Working hard, motivating your team, implementing new structures to deal with change, and so on can reduce anxiety.

Doing a good job, though, tends to offer only long-term relief from anxiety. Games have a quicker effect. This is especially true when many variables in your environment are out of your control. For example, playing No Bad News with a bad or indifferent boss might make your job temporarily less stressful. Playing the Copy game during a tumultuous merger may appear to provide you with protection when you're not sure which boss you're reporting to. Engaging in the Slush Fund game in a down economy may make you feel as if you have a better chance of making your numbers, thus easing your fears of failing to do so.

To Play or Not to Play: That Is the Question

The awareness of games that we talked about in Chapter Five brings with it the possibility of choice: to play or not to play.

How do people in organizations make these decisions? The rational model of decision making is that people look at the pros and cons of different courses of action and assign a positive value to the pros and a negative value to the cons. Then they evaluate the probabilities that the pro will happen, as opposed to the con. On the basis of this evaluation, they make the choice that has the best possible outcome.

The real world is a little less rational than this, so let's look at this decision-making process in practice. Jason, a sales manager for a midsize company in the United States, is "deciding" whether to play the No Bad News and the No Bad

Feedback games. "Deciding" is in quotation marks because Jason isn't consciously thinking about his decision; he simply is thinking about ways to avoid creating more conflict and tension with his boss and his direct reports. More specifically, he is considering using the No Bad News game to avoid passing on negative responses from key customers about the new product launch. Jason is also weighing the possibility of playing the No Bad Feedback game by not telling Petra, a top salesperson until recently, that her performance has slipped over the last six months.

For Jason, the main pro of playing these games is that they allow him to avoid uncomfortable conversations. This is a very personal benefit for him, and the payoff is also quite immediate and quite certain. The cons are that if the product launch continues to go poorly and he remains silent about clients' unhappiness, the company will miss an opportunity to change direction and save the new products; and if he doesn't talk to his salesperson about her slipping performance, she may dig herself in such a hole that Jason will have no other option but to fire her and lose a top talent.

Although the pros and cons may balance each other out, it's easy for someone like Jason to rationalize away the cons and play these games. For instance, he tells himself that the product launch is bound to be successful and that he just has to give it more time, that someone else is bound to tell management that clients are unhappy, that it's better not to risk being the bearer of bad tidings, especially because his boss may suggest that he is in part responsible for the clients' unhappiness. Jason also tells himself that his salesperson is a big girl who knows the score and knows that her bonus and ultimately her job are tied to her performance—that she'll figure things out on her own and return to her old stellar ways.

On the surface, and from Jason's short-term perspective, it seems as if he's making a rational choice. But if we look at the costs and benefits of this decision from a different perspective—a slightly longer time horizon and a slightly less personal bias—his reasoning starts to unravel. The company has been robbed of an opportunity to reevaluate the launch of a key product. An employee has been robbed of an opportunity to recognize and react to her sinking performance. In the longer term, both the supervisor and Petra may lose confidence in Jason; their relationships will probably deteriorate. Jason eventually may still have to have the tough conversations with both of them that he avoided, but those conversations may now be even more difficult as the situations worsen. Jason has missed an opportunity to share his anxieties, and, far from relieving his stress, he has just delayed its onset and potentially magnified its eventual size.

To Play: Opportunistic, Rationalizing, Internalizing

As we've noted, not all decisions take place at a rational level, which means that people like Jason often don't grasp the downside of choosing to play these games. To make the choice not to play, it helps to understand what goes through a person's head as she opts to play and enters into the games going on all around her. We have found that the choice to play can operate at three different levels (our three categories here draw on ideas from the work of Manfred Kets de Vries, 1994, on a related subject).

We refer to the first level as *opportunistic*. When operating at this level, the person realizes that games are going on—he may even realize that they are doing some long-term damage—and he understands that overall, game playing is not the right thing to do. However, he looks for opportunities to cash in on them. At the same time, this choice is somewhat flexible. It's based on how the person perceives reality. If the environment changes—if a new CEO or someone else comes in and makes game playing less attractive—then this individual can adapt to this new reality relatively easily.

The second level is called *rationalizing*. Some people use the "ends justify the means" argument to convince themselves that games are necessary. In other words, a manager chooses to play or facilitate games believing that games are necessary to the smooth functioning of the organization or her group. This individual may engage in an internal pro-versus-con debate, but ends up rationalizing the choice to play games. This choice is more solid than that of the opportunistic game player, but there is still the possibility of moving away from games if circumstances change.

The third level, *internalizing*, is the one at which games are integral to who a manager "is" in the workplace. Unlike the previous two levels, at the internalizing level environmental changes have no impact on this person's decision to play games. Because he has internalized game playing, he now believes it is part of who he is. If a CEO comes in and discourages his favorite games, he'll simply change organizations and find an environment friendlier to these games. In many instances, the person working at the internalizing level has spent his formative years in organizations where intense game playing has been part of the culture.

Not to Play: Exit or Choose Intimacy

Choosing not to play games can take two forms. If you are unwilling to become a player or are uncomfortable with challenging or interrupting the game, one choice is to *exit* the game-playing group or company. Although this option is viable and suggests that you possess strong personal integrity, it is a very tough choice—you're leaving a job and an organization that you may like and that can further your career. You may feel that you're leaving before you achieved what you hoped to achieve. You may be exposing yourself to economic hardship.

The other choice is for *intimacy*, or deep and honest communication, and there are different ways to execute this choice (which we discuss in Chapter Seven). More specifically, when you're faced with the choice of playing or facilitating a game, you decide instead to share your anxieties and needs with another person. It means being completely honest about the changes that are necessary and about how you and another person might work together to make those changes happen. It involves embracing dialogue (and, potentially, conflict) that is not tainted by manipulation.

The risks can involve everything from censure to the loss of the relationship. People may start to view you as not being a team player. You may be seen as overly rigid or straitlaced. So you make yourself vulnerable. And if you stop playing games and start working through these deeper relationships, you may encounter obstacles in the short term. You're trying to get things done by going around the system rather than using the game-based system.

Yet the benefits of making this choice can outweigh the risks when viewed over the long term and from the perspective of the organization. As we saw in Chapter Two, games can gum up the works of many of a company's major processes, from strategic planning to budgeting to leading people. If a sufficient number of individuals in an organization make the choice to play games, these processes will continue to suffer.

One of the best ways we can illustrate this type of choice and its attendant benefits is through the example of a union negotiation. We're using this example because few business interactions involve more game playing than negotiations between labor and management. Keep Them Guessing, Gray Zone, Divide and Conquer, Blame, and Sandbagging are just some of the more common labor negotiation games. Both sides rely on these games to relieve anxiety and meet needs—they seem to represent tried-and-true ways of engaging in conflict and hammering out agreements. Of course, along the way even greater distrust is produced, and both sides may be unhappy with the compromises and manipulation the games require.

Following is a typical game-laden union-management dialogue:

UNION REP: Our position is that we want 10 percent and an increase in vacation time to twenty-five days. The former CEO promised us that.

COMPANY SPOKESPERSON: Don't blame us for what the former CEO promised. His poor decisions are why we can only afford to offer 6 percent. Our data show that this is competitive. We want to maintain vacation time at twenty-three days, and we want the operators to be able to do minor maintenance projects without calling maintenance.

Union Rep: We can't accept this. Our data show that 10 percent is a competitive amount, and the company can afford it. The CEO is getting over 10 percent this year. And we cannot agree to operators doing maintenance, since this clearly falls in the scope of the maintenance department.

And on it goes. No one is being straight about the numbers, and both sides are trying to manipulate. This is as far from an intimate, open dialogue as you can get.

What might that dialogue sound like? How might the union representative and company spokesperson communicate without playing these games? Here is how such a dialogue might go:

Union Rep: We would like to hear from you about what key long-term issues are on the horizon, and what in an ideal world you would like from us. We know that it's important for the company to remain competitive, and we know you understand that our members want to continue to do competitively paid work in a secure environment. So given that, what do you need from us? We can't promise we can do all these things, but let's at least put them on the table.

Company Spokesperson: Thanks. We'll be happy to share our views on this, as well as our reasoning, and we also want your responses to what we present. At the same time, we want to know what really concerns the employees. What are some things that will help keep them motivated and focused and increase our odds of success? You know that our resources are always limited, but with those limitations in mind, we want to allocate the money we do have fairly so that our employees as well as management and our shareholders feel that it's money well spent.

Is it unrealistic to think that two traditional adversaries, such as union and company representatives, can negotiate a contract without games and with openness and honesty? It's only unrealistic if you're cynical and fearful. If you're cynical, you're convinced that the other party will take advantage of your vulnerability. If you're fearful, you believe that people will think you're naive or incompetent.

As he discusses in his book, *Maverick*, Richard Semler (1995), owner and CEO of the Brazilian company Semco, provides an example of how people involved in labor disputes can choose not to play games (or at least minimize them) and can benefit from that choice. During a strike that took place at Semco (strikes provide fertile ground for all types of games), Semler established the following rules:

- Striking employees can continue to come on-site and can continue to use the cafeteria, so long as they do not interfere with anyone who is working.
- No one is punished in any way when he or she decides to return to work.
- No records are kept of who came to work and who led the walkout.
- There is to be no breaking of a picket line.
- Benefits will be fully maintained.
- Respect will be given both to those who decide to continue working and to those who decide to stop.

Semler's rules essentially "banned" many of the games played during union negotiations and strikes. They required that everyone be treated fairly, that there be no hidden agendas during the strike, that the company not be divided into winners and losers. No doubt, Semler recognized that in the short term, these rules might hurt management's negotiating position, but he also knew that by choosing to communicate honestly and openly, he was setting the stage for a stronger union-management relationship, and that is exactly what happened.

A Choice You Make from Your Gut as Much as from Your Mind

Like awakening to game playing, making the choice not to play or promote games is more than a cognitive process. The choice to opt out of game-playing mode has to be heartfelt. You need to make this choice because you're fed up with the games and the damage they do. You also must truly want to operate differently in your work environment and be willing to do whatever is necessary to achieve this goal.

Linda, for instance, is the general manager of the Argentine office of a major consumer goods company. Every August, budget discussions begin, and Linda must propose a budget to her boss, the regional manager, for the following year. Part of the Budget game Linda plays is proposing a sales goal that is a bit higher than the previous year, but not too much higher. Missing the projected target would be devastating to Linda's career, and it would also mean missing out on her bonus.

Linda's friend Peter decided not to play this game, and the result served as a cautionary lesson for Linda. Peter had a similar general manager job, but for the company's Venezuelan office. Convinced that the next year would be terrific, he created a budget that projected sales 50 percent ahead of the current year. Because of a number of external factors over which Peter had no control, his group didn't meet that projected figure, but still came in 40 percent over the previous year and 10 percent above market growth.

Nonetheless, Peter didn't receive his bonus because he missed his target. Even more disturbing, the corporate office began exerting pressure on Peter—monthly reviews, stringent approval procedures for all major expenses—to the point that Peter felt abused by a system that punished those who didn't play the corporate-approved games. As a result, Peter resigned.

Linda went into this particular budget meeting uncertain about playing games, in large part because of her growing concern about integrity. It struck her that she was cheating the company as well as its stakeholders by understating her sales target. She was certain that they could have a great year, but that by settling for a merely good year, she was not doing anyone any favors—including herself. At the same time, when she thought about choosing to have a heart-to-heart discussion with her boss about these issues, she became anxious. Linda had a family to support—she needed the job, and she needed the bonus.

It was only when she arrived home one evening that she was able to make her choice. Her young daughter told her about a story she heard at school that day (it happened to be about a struggling Chinese dancer, but it could have been about many things). As Linda listened to this story, her decision fell in place for her. She realized that she had "no choice"—that this was something she had to do. Linda resolved to have a completely open budget discussion with her boss the next day at work, and she followed through on this promise to herself. The result: Linda and her boss worked out a deal in which Linda set the sales target high. More than that, Linda felt great about clearing the air with her boss— they had a long, rich discussion—and Linda received more support for her various programs than she had expected.

The key point here, though, is that Linda had reached a point in her life where she was ready to choose intimacy over games. She was no longer willing to compromise her integrity. She made a decision about the type of manager and leader she wanted to be, and playing games didn't fit with this definition. The story her daughter told served as a catalyst for her decision, though the catalyst can come from anywhere. We've found that when people choose honest discussion over games, their choice is often triggered by a specific event: a failure or success at work, the departure of a boss or direct report, a personal event (marriage, divorce, birth of a child).

Linda was ready to choose straight talk over games, but not everyone is. Even if you recognize intellectually that games are counterproductive, you need to be ready to take the risk and exhibit the courage that open and honest discussion demands. To determine whether you're at this point, answer the following questions:

Are you aware of and angry about the games played in your group? Is your negative response to games emotional as well as intellectual?

Does it gall you that your group cannot meet more ambitious
goals because of the time and energy wasted on games?
Do you feel as if you're cheating your organization because
you allow these games to flourish?
Do you have a vision of yourself as a manager and a leader
that can't be fulfilled unless you take a stand against
game playing?
Are you able to tolerate the anxiety that you'll probably feel
as you diminish the reliance on games in your group?
Are you willing to take the risk of choosing to manage and
minimize games, even if doing so threatens your job?
Is the time right to make the choice?

This last question is an especially tricky one, as the
following example (based on an article by Collingwood, 2001)
illustrates.

Brenda Gavin, an executive at SmithKline Beecham,
was in charge of the company's house venture fund. Seeing
impressive gains in the company's biotech assets in late 2000,
she wanted to sell these assets to make a significant profit.
Headquarters, however, told her not to sell and that it didn't
want to see a penny more profit in the quarter. Management
wanted to make its numbers, meeting but not exceeding
security analysts' expectations.

The executives were playing the Quarterly Earnings game,
and they expected Brenda to play along. If she were to have
refused, she might have lost her job. From a management
perspective, though, the consequences could have been much
worse. If the company were to make an above-expectations
profit, it might have had trouble meeting that number in the
next quarter. And as everyone knows, when you miss your

numbers by a large amount, the company can lose significant value, which can result in people's losing their jobs.

We're not suggesting from this example that you should use "bad timing" as an excuse to continue playing games. Instead, recognize that if you choose to stop a game, the consequences may be related to what's going on in your company at that particular time. Consider too that it takes courage to see these consequences and still take a stance against a game. For instance, when the company was reformulated as Glaxo-SmithKline, senior financial officers clearly communicated to Brenda that they didn't want her to make bad business decisions just to maintain consistent earnings. They clearly believed that whatever negative consequences might ensue, they weren't as damaging as continuing to keep an artificial lid on profits. Brenda thus received tacit permission to stop playing the Quarterly Earnings game.

We recognize that the time isn't always obviously right (or wrong) when you're faced with a choice about games. Ideally, you'll assess the consequences and decide sooner rather than later to manage the games you or your people are playing.

We also recognize that our "Is the time right?" question is not the only one on the list that is difficult to respond to affirmatively. But if you are able to answer yes to them, you're at a place in your career where you're ready to reduce your dependence on games.

Getting Ready for the Choice: Authenticity and Courage

There is always a certain level of fear in making this choice, as you become vulnerable and are uncertain about the outcomes. So you have to prepare yourself for it. As in running, you strengthen your muscles and practice so that you feel ready when the race comes.

To be ready, you must be confident—making the choice not to play or facilitate games requires guts. So if your identity is dependent on keeping your current job, you won't have the self-confidence to make the call. To acquire this confidence, you must know what you really stand for, your values, purpose, and beliefs—in summary, you must know that your identity is who you are, not what you do. It's development of your character over time that allows you to have independence of thought, and this allows you to choose not to play games, even if you suspect some short-term negatives may result from that choice. In other words, you can put your job at risk by not playing games because your job is not how you define who you are. You're more than your job, and this realization gives you the freedom to be true to your beliefs.

Author and executive coaching guru Kevin Cashman (2008) introduces the concept of character in his book *Leadership from the Inside Out.* He defines leadership as "authentic self-expression that creates value" (p. 20), and this is an ongoing process a leader goes through; we see the choice of interrupting games as a major step of this process.

People who choose not to play or encourage games are always able to speak with an authentic voice. They are able to engage in "courageous conversations" (in the words of poet David Whyte, 2002)—conversations where people take off their masks and make themselves vulnerable. In every organization, leaders exist who are genuine. They earn respect and trust because they communicate without affectation or concern about what others think. While everyone else may be trying to act the way they believe the organization wants them to act, leaders are consistently themselves. It is impossible to be yourself if you're playing a game. If you make the choice not to play, however, you give yourself the chance to lead and manage authentically.

If you and your people actually followed through on these intentions, here is what might happen over the longer term:

- Anxiety levels will go down as more of each team member's needs start to be met; people begin to feel they are being heard; problems are no longer buried or blamed but openly confronted; opportunities are pursued without hidden agendas.
- Deep and continuous dialogue between people saves the group time and money; there are fewer costly surprises; turnover and tension in the group are reduced.
- Open and honest conversations provide a foundation for developing ways of talking about tough issues and sensitive subjects and dealing with them sooner rather than later; over time, intimate dialogues result in people being more energized, more willing to take risks, and motivated to perform at higher levels, all of which translates into better results.

In her poem "The Journey," celebrated poet Mary Oliver (1994) writes that "One day you finally knew/What you had to do, and began." In the next chapter, we will go beyond making the choice (knowing what you have to do) and move to executing the choice (beginning).

CHAPTER 7

Game, Interrupted

Executing Your Choice

Let's begin with a popular quiz. There are five frogs on a log. Three decide to jump off. How many are left?

Five.

Deciding to do something is different than actually doing it.

Let us assume that you have awoken to the games you're playing or facilitating and that you've made the choice against games. This third phase in the process, executing your choice, involves taking actions consistent with what you've decided to do. These actions can vary depending on your level of involvement and your position within the organization. In other words, you may not have been playing games, but you have done nothing to stop them; you may be the CEO with the power to take sweeping action to reduce games throughout your company; or you may be a young professional who can control only games that you or those in your small sphere of influence play.

Obviously, we can't cover every possible game-playing scenario. We can, however, offer advice that you can adapt to your particular situation. We've found that even after people become aware of games within their company and made the decision to stop participating or facilitating, it can be a challenge to take action against them. When games are integrated deeply into the culture, it is difficult to separate them from the whole and target the games (and avoid hitting the good parts of the company).

Thus people often have the best of intentions regarding games but don't take any action. This chapter is designed to help avoid this possibility. We'll provide step-by-step instructions for this third phase of our ACE method. First, though, we want to place our action steps in a larger conceptual context.

Positive and Negative Forces: Increase One, Decrease the Other

Force field analysis provides the perfect framework for understanding the two types of actions you can take against games. This framework was posited by social scientist Kurt Lewin (n.d.), and it helps explain the various forces in play during social situations. Some forces drive movement toward a specific objective (helping forces); others block movement toward this objective (hindering forces). Lewin theorized that to change a social system, you must both strengthen the helping forces and reduce the impact of hindering forces.

Using force field analysis to change the organizational game-playing social system, we came up with the diagram in Figure 7.1. As you can see, in order to achieve higher performance, increased creativity and risk taking, and a more

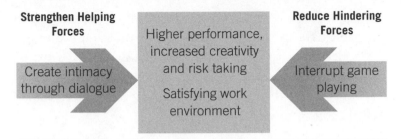

FIGURE 7.1 Force Field Analysis Applied to the Organizational Game-Playing Social System

satisfying work environment, you must reduce the hindering forces, which entails interrupting the game, while also bolstering the helping forces, which means creating intimacy through dialogue. Let's start by talking about what you can do to interrupt games.

Interrupting: Knowing the Points Where You Can Intervene

Earlier, we described a variety of games and how they unfold. When you think about the games played in your company, you may have trouble breaking each game's progression into a series of steps. It's difficult to know where the Boss Said game starts and ends, for instance, because this game-playing behavior is enmeshed in the routines of the workday and the various modes of communication used in your company—e-mails, phone calls, conversations. It's difficult, therefore, to sort out when a manager starts the game by invoking the name of the CEO, as she may have alluded to it in an e-mail, reinforced it in a phone call, and then really drew everyone's attention to the CEO's statement during a meeting. Looking back, it may also be challenging to re-create the progression of the game unless you concentrate on how the game evolved.

Nonetheless, to interrupt a game effectively, it helps to think about it in terms of discrete steps. In his book *What Do You Say After You Say Hello?* Eric Berne (1972) describes games as following a six-step sequence:

1. The Con. The opening line that invites the other person into the game.
2. The Gimmick. The other person's interest in the Con.
3. The Response. The normal back-and-forth interaction of the game that can last for a period of time.
4. The Switch. Something is said that disturbs the back-and-forth interaction.
5. The Cross Up. A sense of unease that all is not as it seems.
6. The Payoff. The reason (which may be unconscious) for someone to play the game.

Now let's look at these six steps as they play out in a common business game. If you recall, the Sandbagging game involves understating financial projections during budget discussions. Carla, the general manager for Mexico of a multinational company, makes a budget presentation to her boss, Sergio, head of Latin America, and Alex, the region CFO. Carla is well aware of how this game is played, and though she doesn't like it, she goes along with it. Carla knows she must choose a figure that is achievable, as her bonus and those of her people depend on making their numbers. At the same time, it can't be too low or it will dampen Sergio's and Alex's enthusiasm for funding her team's efforts. Carla decides on stating that revenues will increase by 12 percent, though she knows 15 to 16 percent is a realistic target.

Carla's conversation with Sergio and Alex, followed by a brief translation of each statement as it relates to a game-playing step, goes as follows:

CARLA (THE CON): We've really tried to put together an aggressive proposal, but as you know, conditions in Mexico will also be challenging next year with the elections, and there will be some softening in sector A.

Translation: Carla is expressing false caution. She is inviting Sergio and Alex to play along with her overly pessimistic view.

SERGIO (THE GIMMICK): We recognize that. However, the U.S. is going through a trough, and we need to pull out all the stops in our region.

Translation: Sergio is picking up on the Con and taking the other extreme position in order to create an acceptable compromise.

ALEX (THE RESPONSE, PART 1): Your margin looks weak in Q3 next year, compared to Q3 this year.
CARLA (THE RESPONSE, PART 2): This is because we are unable to offset the union wage increase with increased revenue.

Translation: Alex's main goal is to push Carla and see how hard she'll push back. Carla continues with her excuse-making, pessimistic view, ignoring all the positive developments. They will go back and forth like this until Sergio makes the Switch.

SERGIO (THE SWITCH): Carla, I'm afraid a revenue increase of 12 percent in what is fundamentally a healthy market is just not acceptable. You need to set your sights at 15 percent or more.

Translation: Sergio suspects that Carla is sandbagging and has underestimated how well they might do in the coming year, but he is unsure of the extent to which she has underestimated. By saying Carla's figure is unacceptable, he is making a break from the back-and-forth discussion.

ALEX (THE CROSS UP): I didn't realize that you [Carla] thought that next year was going to be so tough. Frankly, I'm surprised.

Translation: Alex is communicating to Carla that he's bothered that Carla is taking such a negative view on the year, hoping to use this as leverage to get her to up her numbers.

CARLA (THE PAYOFF): Okay, let's say 13 percent, but I don't want you to think it's going to be easy, and remember that I cautioned you. But I guarantee we'll do our best to make this number.

Translation: Carla got what she wanted, but she's pretending that 13 percent is an overly ambitious number so that when they hit it on the nose, everyone will be pleased that she made her ambitious objective.

Be aware that in real organizational life, this dialogue is not so concise, and the game can be played in all sorts of ways besides through one conversation. Our point here is to demonstrate that games tend to be sequential and that you can call a halt to them at any one of these distinct steps. In other words, you refuse to go on to the next step. Carla, for instance, can refuse to offer the Con, her falsely pessimistic statement about the upcoming year. Sergio can refuse to take the bait and initiate the Gimmick—instead of telling Carla that they have to pull out all the stops next year (which they don't really have to do), he can be honest about what the company really needs from the Mexico group.

We believe it's a useful exercise to try to identify the progression of games in your group. This helps you recognize how games start, gain momentum, draw people deeper into the game's mechanics, and ultimately provide a player with a payoff (and another player with a loss, at least in some instances).

To call a halt to the game, though, you can simply divide the game into a beginning, a middle, and an end, and use these three points as opportunities to interrupt the game. If you take action at the beginning, you're refusing to start the game or participate when someone else tries to start it. If you interrupt it in the middle, you're calling a time-out in the middle of the game, communicating that you don't want to continue playing. If you interrupt the game at the end, it signifies that you're refusing the payoff—you turn down the "in" with your boss, the artificially deflated budget number, the demotion of a rival, or whatever form your win might have taken.

Recognizing when and how you can interrupt creates options—options that may suit your particular situation and increase the odds that you'll interrupt the game. You can also use these guidelines to coach your people in how to withdraw from game playing. They have the same options to disengage that you do, and if you can raise their awareness and communicate to them that they have real choices in this regard, they may decide to exercise those options.

The Steps for Interrupting a Game

We know that it's difficult to interrupt a game, especially if it's one that is deeply embedded in a culture and that employees in a particular group have played for a sustained period of time. One manager, Maarten, who works for a large organization where the Gotcha and Gossip games are endemic, noted that he tried to interrupt the games in the beginning, the middle, *and* the end, but was thwarted each time. When one of his colleagues started a conversation with him about how an individual in their group had overlooked a memo and angered their boss by doing exactly what the memo instructed not to do, Maarten refused to talk about it, making an excuse that he had something else to do. When this person again started talking to him about the third individual—telling Maarten that this was an opportunity for them to edge him out of a new team that was forming— Maarten began a discussion in which he talked about how he didn't think that his colleague was being fair and that he was using a relatively common and inconsequential mistake to tar and feather this other individual.

The game went on, and even when Maarten refused to take advantage of this mistake for his own personal gain—he was up for membership on the aforementioned team, and refused to bring up the mistake—his colleague and others continued to play Gossip and Gotcha. Just as disturbing, people continued to invite Maarten in to these games, and he felt his resistance to them weaken. As much as he wanted to interrupt them, it seemed to require a lot of energy and courage, and his efforts didn't seem to have much effect.

Part of the problem is that interrupting a game is as much an art as it is a science. The following steps, therefore, are designed to help you increase the effectiveness of your interruptions.

Step 1: Write the Sequence of Stages for the Game

Writing a game sequence can be a bit challenging because, as we noted, games don't always immediately fall neatly into Berne's six stages. For this reason, use the following questions to help you chart how your actions evolve and mirror different aspects of the game:

How are you inviting the other person into the game? Are you saying or doing something that encourages others to participate? Are you initiating the action of the game, or are you saying or doing something in response to another person's invitation that helps launch the game?

What is the other person's response to your game-initiating words or deeds? How does he foster game energy and involvement through this response?

As the game moves forward, what is the typical ongoing back-and-forth between you and the other player? What types of conversations do you have that epitomize the game? What types of actions do you both take in concert that typify the game?

What disturbs the game or moves it to another level? What happens that raises the game stakes or causes the game to veer in a new, higher-impact direction?

Can you describe the sense of unease the game creates? How does it foster feelings of paranoia, anger, anxiety, defensiveness, fear, shame, guilt, and so on?

What is the game's payoff? Can you describe what you receive for playing the game effectively? Can you describe what another person might lose?

Step 2: Identify Where and How It Would Be Easiest for You to Interrupt the Game

Think about the best point at which to stop the game's natural progression, and how you would prefer to do so. Give yourself options for action, and rehearse how each option might unfold in a real-life scenario:

How can you stop inviting the other person into the game?

What might you do so that the other individual loses interest in the game?

What might you say or do to stop the back-and-forth routine of the game? Could you "call" the game or take on a role that is different from the familiar one that you assume as part of the game?

Can you do something that would stop the game from moving from one level to the next? Can you prevent the game from progressing and cause it to become stuck in back-and-forth mode until it naturally ends? Can you simply withdraw from playing the game?

Can you capitalize on the sense of unease to raise awareness of the game and stop it?

Are you willing to give up the payoff to interrupt the game?

Step 3: Act When the Moment Is Right

To interrupt the game, you have to do something. The first two steps should have given you a sense of when and how it would be best for you to interrupt. What you actually do, however, will probably be a product of your management style, your personality, and the culture in which you operate. You may choose to take immediate, overt action at a game's inception or instead choose to interrupt in a more subtle manner later on. The key is to interrupt, and here are some options for doing so:

- Choose to play a different role than the one the game calls for (thereby disrupting the game).
- Call the game—call other people's attention to the fact that you are both playing a game, describing what it is and how it's counterproductive.
- Undermine the game—say or do something that robs people of their motivation for playing. For example, the boss can stop the Copy game by saying, "Could you please deal directly with Ms. X? And you don't need to copy me anymore on this sort of correspondence."
- Bring in another person (your boss, the CEO, a coach) to help stop the game.
- Exit—remove yourself from a game-playing situation, transfer out of a game-playing group, or even resign from the company.

Taking any of these actions involves overcoming obstacles—both situational and psychological—that can discourage you from interrupting a game. It's possible that in the short term, you'll receive negative feedback. In some cultures, games are so endemic that people resent it when someone interrupts the action. In these situations, interrupters are viewed as being "difficult," not going along with the program, or not a good fit. Some people's anxiety increases when they bow out of a game. Even if no one says anything to them, they fret about the consequences of calling a game or bringing in another person to disrupt it.

In the long run, however, game interruptions are beneficial, both for the individual and the group. People feel good about having the courage to break from the game, regardless of whether it is sooner or later in its progression. More than that, if they're able to diminish the game playing in their group, they see a resurgence of energy and creativity that can be marshaled to accomplish real business goals.

■■

We'd like to share a story that illustrates what happens when people take action to interrupt games.

Nancy, a midlevel manager at a midsize insurance company, supervised twenty people in a division office that was hundreds of miles from the company's headquarters. A number of games were played in the organization and in Nancy's group, the most prominent of which was the Copy game. Typically, people in Nancy's group played this game to cover themselves ("I e-mailed everyone about my plan, so ...") or to imply that others were to blame for mistakes. Over the years, Nancy had grown accustomed to a slew of e-mails being sent whenever something went wrong—a quota wasn't met, a high-potential suddenly quit to join a competitor, a costly mistake was made. When Nancy's group went over budget implementing a new corporate policy, e-mails flew out of her group, rationalizing the overspending and blaming various individuals. Naturally, Nancy's boss as well as her boss's boss were copied on these e-mails.

In the middle of these e-mail exchanges, Nancy decided to call the game. More specifically, Nancy received an e-mail from one of her direct reports indicating that she had warned Nancy of potential cost overruns months ago. She didn't directly blame Nancy for not listening to her—she admitted that at the time the overruns seemed insignificant—but she was e-mailing to alert senior management to her foresight.

Nancy was fed up. A number of events in her personal life were having an impact on how she viewed her job. Recently divorced and having just sent her third and youngest child off to college, she had gained perspective and courage by dealing with these life events. As a result, she was no longer willing to play games. So Nancy called a meeting with her three top people and told them that she felt the Copy game was out of control and that some people were devoting more time to it than to their real work. At first, her people objected to Nancy's calling the game, justifying this behavior by saying that it was important to keep everyone in the information loop. Nancy disagreed, and, after some conversation with the team, they reached agreement on a new policy regarding e-mails that placed restrictions on who was copied on what type of e-mail. At first, her people resented this restriction and thought it a poor decision, especially from a political standpoint. Within six months, however, people adjusted to the new policy and found that e-mailing had ceased to take up as much of their time. Perhaps more important, they didn't devote as much creativity or invest as much effort in crafting e-mails as they once had. In fact, they spent more time communicating by phone or in person, and the relationships in the group strengthened. With the decrease in the playing of the Copy game came an increase in trust among group members.

The Steps Toward Open and Ongoing Dialogue

As Figure 7.1 shows, interrupting is a way to counter the negative forces that drive games. Interrupting is only half the solution, however. If you don't deal with the anxiety that throws people into game playing, you may slip back into game-playing mode at some point in the future. Interrupting the game in a sustainable way should be your goal, and you can achieve it if you are willing to talk openly about the needs that underlie the games. In other words, you and your people should feel free to point out when games are being played, to question the impact within your group and in the organization as a whole, and to maintain an ongoing dialogue about the underlying needs that the games are meeting. The head of one entrepreneurial organization put it well when he said, "Honesty, transparency, and communication are how to deal with games. The more games are played, the less honesty, transparency, and communication."

With that thought in mind, let's examine the two steps that are helping forces in achieving higher performance, increased creativity, and a more satisfying work environment by facilitating anxiety-reducing dialogue.

Step 1: Initiate Tough Conversations

By tough, we mean conversations that make you, the other person, or both of you uncomfortable. No one likes to admit that she has been manipulating another person or has hidden agendas. Few managers enjoy confronting their people and telling them they've been wasting time and energy blaming others or trying to use a boss's utterances to get what they want. It is even tougher to grapple with your own anxiety and that of others in a transparent conversation. Yet this is the only way you're going to battle that anxiety to a draw, to counter it as a catalyst for games. To that end, here are suggestions for how to initiate and carry on dialogues that require the openness and honesty that we define as intimacy.

Before the conversation, prepare yourself in the following ways:

- *Adopt a learning stance.* In other words, don't get stuck on what you need to teach the other person or on being defensive, but instead open yourself up to learning what the other person has to say. The more open minded you are and the less you try to convince the other person that he's wrong, the better the conversation will go. It's more important to learn why the other individual plays the game than to chastise him for playing it. So prior to sitting down with someone and having a games talk, tell yourself that learning is your priority.
- *Focus on the facts.* Before your conversation, reflect on the mechanics of the game. Identify the actions that made up the game. Then review in your own mind (or write it out on a piece of paper) how you viewed the game—how

you perceived what was happening. Next, detail how it played out in a business situation. In doing these things, recognize that games can be seen very differently by different players, considering that games are linked to the player's intention. You may find that a person was playing the Boss Said game during her presentation, whereas the person you're about to have a conversation with may believe that she was just representing what the CEO really expected and had expressed in a previous private meeting. In setting forth the facts in your own mind, you can at least be clear about what you think is going on when games are played.

- *Identify your real needs.* Remember that games are just a way to address the anxiety that comes from not having a real need met, and that the purpose of the conversation is to find another way to meet that real need. For that purpose, an important step is to identify what need or needs you are attempting to meet through your game playing.

- *Consider how games affect your identity.* Some games may make you think you're competent at your job. Others foster a sense of belonging. Recognize that you need to consider how your perception of your identity will be affected when the game is interrupted. Prepare to discuss this identity issue.

- *Choose a time, a place, and a person with whom to share what you have understood about your rationale for playing games.* Ideally, you'll choose your main game-playing partner or the person in your group who frequently initiates games. Think about what you're going to say and how you're going to say it. Resolve to communicate how games allay your anxiety—how you as well as others gravitate toward games rather than facing issues head-on.

During the conversation, focus on the following behaviors:

- *Talk about the facts, about how the anxiety in your workplace is driving you or others to play games, about the real needs you have identified, and about how the game affects your identity.* Focus on how everything from fears of being downsized out of a job to concerns about a new CEO's policies are causing you to play specific games. Consider what your vulnerabilities are and how workplace issues or industry volatility pushes you to play games to relieve this anxiety. What is your real need? Does the game function as a protection or a diversion? Does it give you a sense of power and control? Does it provide you with a sense of achievement? Being able to talk about these issues will generate the intimacy required to find together an alternative solution to address the real needs.
- *Create an ongoing dialogue.* In this dialogue, you both talk and listen; you are honest and open about your game-playing role, and you invite the other person to respond in kind. You use such dialogue skills as listening; respecting others as legitimate, whatever their opinion is; suspending your opinion and the certainty that lies behind it; and voicing your truth. The key is to dig down beneath the game playing and get to the core issues that concern both of you—the

company's dramatic changes in policy and process, the increasing competitiveness of the industry, job uncertainty, the stretch assignments that lie ahead. Talking honestly and continuously about these issues diminishes anxiety as well as the need to play games.

- *Look for the "third story."* If you have one perspective on the situation and your conversation partner has another, see if you can arrive at a consensus about it based on your two stories and feelings. Remember to keep a learning stance.

- *Find an alternative solution.* As you have both expressed your real needs and better understood each other, find together an alternative way to address those needs, to reduce anxiety in a non-gaming way. Commit to your choice to stop playing games and discuss ways to keep the intimate dialogue going.

Sean is a senior manager at a large organization; he was brought in about a year ago from another company because of "his reputation as a thought leader and his ability to translate those thoughts into actions." At this previous job, Sean had helped flatten the company in order to foster quicker decisions and more innovation, and his efforts had helped that company achieve significant success in their marketplace. Reina, the CEO who brought him over, hoped that Sean would demonstrate the same turnaround expertise with their struggling organization.

At this new organization, however, Sean assessed the situation and realized that the best strategy was to move slowly and incrementally. Although he made some changes, many of his moves were subtle and long term in impact. Sean found himself under pressure from Reina and other senior leaders to effect a major turnaround quickly. As Sean became increasingly anxious, he also became increasingly drawn into various organizational games.

At first, Sean had tried to tell Reina about the problems that he observed: that they needed fresh talent with different capabilities than those the current staff possessed; that the bureaucracy was entrenched and would take a while to be reworked into a more flexible, responsive structure; that the company's financial resources were being sapped by a lawsuit and by heavy investment in a new technology. But Reina and other leaders of the company didn't really hear what Sean had to say. In fact, they would ask him why he was being so pessimistic and tell him that "this is a much more positive company than the one you used to work for." Eventually, he got the message and started playing No Bad News. He learned that by sugarcoating bad news and hyperbolizing good news, he received more approval from Reina and other senior people, and pressure for a quick turnaround diminished.

Similarly, he discovered that if he periodically introduced a new idea into the organizational system with a lot of fanfare, that too would relieve the pressure. Sean became skilled at Big Splash Career Hopper, using slick PowerPoint presentations to make a case for his latest innovation and the promise it held for the organization's renaissance. Sean knew that none of these ideas were going to achieve the ambitious goals Reina had set, but he also knew that they maintained the illusion that the company was moving in the right direction and that the turnaround was just around the corner.

After about a year of playing these games, though, Sean had had it. He interrupted the games during step 6—the

Payoff. Reina had called Sean into her office to tell him how pleased she was with his latest idea, and that she was giving him a raise and a promotion. All at once, the hypocrisy of his game playing hit Sean hard. Ironically, he had been able to tolerate this hypocrisy until he was to be rewarded for it.

He called the game, telling Reina that he believed the culture encouraged game playing and that it had a tremendously counterproductive impact on productivity. Sean wasn't hostile or even angry as he talked to Reina about the pressure he believed he was under and how it funneled him directly to the games the culture endorsed. He was respectful of the company and what Reina and her people had managed to build, and he listened carefully to Reina's defense of that culture.

More than anything else, Sean was honest and open about how he felt. Reina couldn't miss the authenticity in Sean's tone and in what he said. Because she respected Sean, she listened carefully, and at the end of their two-hour conversation, she respected Sean even more for his honesty. Although she didn't agree with everything Sean told her, she realized that the games Sean named did exist, and that they had spiraled out of control. Reina promised that she would do something.

It's important to note that although this conversation wasn't a panacea, it represented the first of many between Sean and Reina, and over time their ability to speak to each other with great transparency and without hidden agendas helped them manage the games that they used to play together. They were able to uncover a series of games played in the organization (the ecology of games we will describe in the next chapter) and address them over time. They became a much more productive, effective team as they substituted straight talk for games, and within two years they had achieved a modest turnaround for the company—not as significant as Reina had hoped for, but still something they both could be proud of.

Step 2: Come to Terms with Your Feelings

Interrupting a game and choosing open, honest dialogue over games are not just cognitive experiences. Sean, for instance, deliberately made himself more vulnerable in the presence of a boss than he had ever done before, and this was scary. As he talked (and later when he had time to reflect on the conversation), he was sad that he had wasted so much time going along with the games rather than confronting the issues head-on. He was able to forgive himself and to focus his energy in moving forward. That first conversation and subsequent ones with Reina were truly meaningful experiences. In fact, a bond of trust was forged from these conversations, and that was a tremendously rewarding feeling.

Acknowledge and accept these feelings rather than allow them to scare you. If you let your emotions get the better of you, they can intensify the anxiety that caused you to turn to games in the first place. Some people become overly fearful about interrupting a game. Others dislike the vulnerable feelings that open, honest conversations engender. Still others feel uncertain about how effective they can be as leaders or managers without games to lean on.

These feelings are perfectly natural, but unless you accept them and articulate them, they can undermine your best intentions not to play or facilitate games. Whether with a boss, a coach, or a colleague, express how you feel about interrupting the game and initiating a dialogue. Talk about your positive as well as your negative feelings. Don't try to be a "tough guy (or gal)." The process of withdrawing from games is emotional for everyone, and acknowledging these emotions to yourself and others is another step away from games. Then using the energy contained in these same "negative" emotions as input for an open and honest dialogue is the best you can do in creating a truly positive and "intimate" game-free relationship.

CHAPTER 8

Interconnections
How Games Are Linked
In to an Ecology

In Chapters Five through Seven, we presented a method for dealing with games at the level of the individual. As a manager, you may be playing games or facilitating them, but your ability to control them depends on examining your own attitudes and actions related to these games. Through Awakening, Choice, and Execution, you can act to diminish the number of games in your work or in your area.

Games exist in a larger context, however, and people learn to play games through interaction with their environments. Senior figures in an organization have parent-like authority, and just as kids learn certain psychological games from their mom and dad, so too do employees learn certain games from their leaders and other executives. In fact, the game-playing environment is influenced by organizational traditions and history, organizational traumas, new CEOs, relationships with suppliers and customers, and innumerable other factors.

From all this, companies build up patterns of games—specific configurations of linked games. These games have their source in what we call organizational game DNA—a deeply embedded corporate theme that influences the games people in a given company typically play. Toward the end of the chapter, we'll identify four common DNA types.

Understanding the interdependency of games played in your company is especially critical for organizational change purposes. But understanding the ecology of games is also important for how you run your group. What do we mean by ecology of games? In the Merriam-Webster dictionary, ecology is defined as a branch of science concerned with the interrelationship of organisms and their environments and as the totality or pattern of relations between organisms and their environment.

Working with this definition, we view the ecology of games as a pattern of interlocking games that exist in a given system (for example, an organization). This definition also suggests that games reinforce each other and create the type of environment where these games can flourish and spread.

In attempting to get a handle on games played in your area, you need to be aware of the larger context. It may be that certain games have been institutionalized—they've been played for many years and are part of the culture—so you may face a greater challenge trying to get them under control. Other games played in your group may be of more recent vintage or less connected to the main game ecology in your company; these will probably be easier to deal with. As you wrestle with games, it helps to know how the games played are connected and part of a larger framework and how one type of game feeds another. You can then be alert for a particular combination of games and address more than one when you use the ACE method.

To help you see what the ecology of games involves, let's look at one particular company, which we'll call Bionic.

The Invisible Links Between Connected Games

As we noted earlier, it can be difficult to "see" a game in all its aspects at first glance because it is so much a part of the work routine. You don't notice the game's starting point, midpoint, or payoff because it isn't structured like traditional games. A bell doesn't ring announcing the game's start; the game isn't divided into timed quarters; no distinct end point exists. Similarly, you may not see the links between games initially. It may not be apparent how the Gossip game, for example, is a perfect complement to the Sandbagging game—how by purposely spreading "inside information" that a new product's prospects don't look promising or that a highly effective division head might take early retirement, you can more easily convince headquarters that a lower estimate of earnings is justified, and then look like a hero when you exceed the budget. Even though these games are in different categories—Interpersonal and Budget—they can still be connected.

At Bionic Corporation, the following games are played with some frequency:

- Gotcha
- Copy
- Gossip
- The Boss Said
- Gray Zone
- Token Involvement
- Outsourcing Management to Consultants
- Victim

These games form an ecology at Bionic because each game subtly reinforces others. Gotcha is played because of the unstated but widespread belief that errors are the source of major organizational problems and that exposing other people's mistakes is appropriate and effective work behavior. In turn, Copy and the Boss Said are played protectively in response to Gotcha: "I was only following the CEO's policy; if that results in a cost overrun, don't blame me." Similarly, Gray Zone also shields people from blame, in that accountability is unclear.

All these games foster a sense of victimization (Victim game). When people are so busy accusing others and protecting themselves, they generate feelings of disempowerment—people really don't believe that they have much control over what happens, and they assume that what happens probably won't be good for them. When things go wrong, employees feel powerless and taken advantage of by fate, management, or other forces outside their control.

For this reason, when Bionic's leadership launched an organizational initiative designed to energize and motivate people by pushing decision-making downward, most employees reacted as if management were playing the Token Involvement game. They simply assumed that the company wanted to push the blame down to line employees when things went wrong, but retain all the real decision-making power at the top.

Outsourcing Management to Consultants also flows from the sense of victimization, as management believes that their people really aren't capable of handling critical assignments. They outsource tasks that used to be handled in-house to high-priced consultants who are viewed as better able to handle tasks primarily because they're not employees and, therefore, somehow more trustworthy and competent.

Finally, all the defensiveness, victimization, and blaming stirs up rumors and innuendo. People whisper about who's in and who's out, who is going to take the fall for a failed project and who is likely to sail through. The more people gossip about who screwed up, the more that managers play Gotcha. The ecology provides the energy and motivation to play games harder and more often. It's easy for managers to get trapped in the connected web of games, as Figure 8.1 suggests:

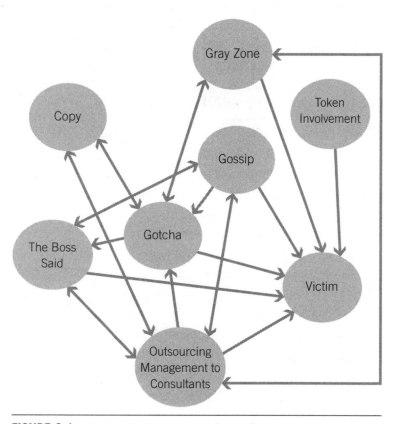

FIGURE 8.1 Bionic Corporation Ecology of Games

Being aware of all the connections between games can help organizations better deal with them. As these connections indicate, singling out one game for neutralization won't work. Tackling the Gotcha game on its own, for example, will be difficult when games like the Boss Said and Gossip are pervasive. People often simply take the games "underground," playing them subtly. Instead of accusing a direct report of making a mistake, the subtle manager frames his accusation as "positive feedback." The manager may even say, "I'm not telling you that you made a mistake," when in fact that's exactly what he's saying—he has simply sugarcoated his remarks.

Identifying Your Game Ecology

As you start identifying the prevalent game ecology in your company, you must understand the interrelated nature of your organization's games and map them visually. To help you diagram this ecology, we will rely on the tools of systems thinking (such as feedback, causal loop diagrams, and archetypes) as presented by Peter Senge and his MIT colleagues (1984) in *The Fifth Discipline Fieldbook*. We will try to translate these tools into simple actions and steps that you can use to map the games that are played in your company (or within your group or area).

Start by focusing on the game that's played the most. Draw a circle in the middle of a piece of paper with the name of this "central" game written inside the circle.

Now determine what other games are related to this central game. (Refer to Chapter One for our list of most common games or to the Appendix for both that list and the supplemental list.) To make this determination, ask the following questions:

What type of atmosphere is created by this central game? Does it cause people to be suspicious, defensive, political, secretive? What other games cause people to react in similar ways?

Can you find a causal link between this central game and at least one other game? That is, can you create a statement such as, "If we play central game A, we naturally will play game B because . . ."?

What is the benefit of the central game to players? (For example, the Boss Says game has the benefit of justifying your actions.) What other game or games have similar goals?

Using the answers to these questions, delineate links to other relevant games using lines and circles with the games' names written within the circles.

For all the first-tier "satellite" games you identified, go through the previous questions and see if you can create a second tier of games. Specifically, for each satellite game, determine what other games might naturally follow. You may discover that a given game spawns yet another tier of supporting games.

The goal of this exercise is to help you see the ecology or game system from a step-back perspective. You shouldn't feel you need to create the perfect map and identify every game no matter how minor or how far removed from your group. You simply want to create a general diagram that illustrates the various linkages between key games.

A Diagnostic for the Game-Playing Aspect of a Culture

The diagram you create provides you with all sorts of useful information—information that may not be apparent at first. But once you have your diagram in place, you can use it to dig below the surface and explore the people, policies, traditions, and other factors that keep game playing alive and well in your company.

In the following paragraphs, we offer a series of steps you can use to turn your game ecology diagram into a diagnostic. After each step, we present an example of how this was done by one manager who completed the exercise:

1. See if you can identify patterns of game playing within your ecology. For instance, think about when in the past year games were played at peak levels. Did these peaks coincide with anxiety-producing events, such as a downturn in the economy or a merger or acquisition? Another pattern might involve a high incidence of games in one area of the company and a low incidence in another. A third pattern may be that certain types of games cluster in one organizational group, whereas other types cluster in another area.

Example: "The biggest pattern in our organization: spikes in playing of No Bad News, No Decision and Kill the Messenger games during bad quarters—everyone is afraid to say anything negative or make decisions during these times, and if someone does deliver bad news, they're viewed as being overly negative. These games seem to recur primarily below the senior level. The leaders in our company tend to play

Keep Them Guessing, which only exacerbates game playing at lower levels."

2. Create a history of how your game ecology evolved. What was the rough chronology for the games and how games began to merge? How did people playing the central game begin to engage in other types of games until the games all seemed to blend together?

Example: "The central game, No Bad News, really began being played in earnest about eight years ago when the organization went through a terrible period. Our CEO at the time was heavily invested in a spinoff dot-com business that was hurt by the dot-com bust and eventually went under. A new CEO came in, then left within a year, and a new guy was brought in who was an advocate of positive mental attitude. He felt a lot of the company's problems were a self-fulfilling prophecy—we think the worst, and then the worst happens. Though he left a year ago, his legacy has been all the games related to being relentlessly positive."

3. Describe your company's "parallel universe"—how people are doing job tasks, but at the same time, there's a game subtext behind the way in which they perform these tasks.

Example: "People meet as part of their teams or in their functional groups, and team leaders seem to be trying to move people toward consensus and action, but they're just orchestrating elaborate ways of not making decisions. During one recent team meeting, the team leader spent weeks researching two options, soliciting our opinions and then finally focused on the option that seemed best. Then he wrote a white paper related to this option and disseminated it through the organization. Then he received feedback which caused him to go back to the drawing board and decide this option wasn't right for the time being."

Organizational Games DNA

The game ecology in your organization has a source. It didn't just appear out of the blue. For some organizations, the source can be traced back many years, even all the way back to the company's origins and its founders. More commonly, the ecology started forming after a singularly important event, such as a CEO's being appointed and remaking the company in his image, or in the leaders' responses at a moment of great crisis (a financial collapse or environmental disaster, for example). The games most commonly played in your company have a genetic imprint, and the parent is usually a leader who made the company what it is today.

In fact, if you ask the question, "Who created the policies, processes, and culture that dominate our organization?" you can probably figure out when the DNA was created and how it evolved.

The more important question, though, is what this DNA consists of. Identifying the core DNA material behind your games offers great insight into why your organization plays the games it does. Many times, people look at the particular mix of games we describe, and wonder what made these specific games rise to the surface in their companies. At first, the collection seems completely random. It is not necessarily related to the type of industry (there is no packaged goods game ecology, for instance, or any game groups dictated by a particular type of business). The tendency is to assume that people in your company play the Pre-Deal game much more than the Gray Zone game for no particular reason other than that the former caught on and the latter never did.

But the way games evolve into an ecology isn't random. They coalesce around a theme. More specifically, a particular driving belief or norm spawns a specific grouping of games.

In the Gerund Company, a midsize manufacturer, for instance, this overarching belief is *People aren't trustworthy*. This isn't a belief that anyone articulates in so many words. In fact, the CEO and other senior leaders would insist that trust is part of the cultural fabric. Yet this CEO and his top people tend to view their employees cynically and pessimistically. This attitude has its roots in the company's history, one marked by labor-management strife. Management has always viewed labor's motives with suspicion, and vice versa. This attitude has spread beyond the traditional labor-management borders. Middle managers in the IT department and finance also share the unspoken belief that people are not trustworthy. As evidence, the company's systems and processes have a much greater than normal number of monitoring devices: tight performance management processes, deep-reaching audit functions, punitive consequences when mistakes are caught, massive key performance indicators exercises, and so on. The underlying assumption is that people aren't careful or will deliberately sabotage an initiative they dislike.

More to the point, the games people play reflect this theme of distrust. The Gotcha game is the central one played at Gerund. Mistakes are pointed out frequently and sometimes maliciously. Nitpicking is common, and there is a sense that managers are looking over one's shoulder. It follows that if people are not trustworthy, managers must be constantly vigilant for mistakes. The Victim game is extremely popular among employees. Not only is it a logical reaction to Gotcha—I screwed up because my boss is always picking on me—but it has deeper roots in the "people aren't trustworthy" mantra. If no one trusts you, how can you possibly do a good job? No matter what you do, it won't be good enough. In turn, the Window Watcher game is a favorite among managers who, rather than fire someone who acts like a victim, shuttles her to the side, giving her boring, meaningless tasks. The Window Watcher game essentially says to the victim: You think things are bad now? Try shuffling paper clips eight hours a day for the next few years.

Again, the Window Watcher game fits the untrustworthiness theme—after all, if people can't be trusted, they might as well be assigned to jobs where they can do no harm.

■■

Following are descriptions of four of the most common organizational game DNAs and their main themes:

• *Mistrusting.* As the previous example indicated, suspiciousness and even paranoia characterize this strand of DNA. Leaders tend to believe that people are incompetent and will make mistakes through laziness, lack of skill, or stupidity. They value processes and consultants over their own people and attempt to keep their best and brightest through compensation packages alone, believing that such things as meaningful work, development opportunities, and flexible work schedules are not important. Most employees are unwilling to take risks because of management attitudes, and they often are defensive in response to even mildly critical suggestions. They do not believe what their bosses say and take every promise with a grain of salt. Games frequently played as a function of this DNA include Gotcha, Victim, Window Watcher, Gray Zone, and Blame.

• *Exclusive.* Here the theme is that an inner circle exists, and everyone else is on the outside looking in. In other words, a relatively small group is considered the organization's power brokers, and if you aren't a member of this group or don't have connections to it, you're pretty much out of luck. As a result of this mind-set, a minority of the organization's employees are treated well, and a majority are not. The latter group struggles to obtain needed resources, get pay raises, and stay in the information loop.

In some cases, the company is clearly divided into haves and have-nots; it is seen as clubby and elitist, and a huge gap exists between these two groups. Employees are told what to do, and their ideas are rarely solicited. Other times, this DNA shows up very subtly: all employees seem to be equal, but when it comes to the important stuff, there is a small group of preferred loyal people (for example, family members, homegrown people, friends of the founder, compatriots of the CEO, and so on) who, independently of their roles and responsibilities, are called on for opinions and decisions. The downside of this DNA is that merit can take a back seat to connections. Games frequently played as part of this DNA include the Boss Said, Marginalize, Pre-Deal, Token Involvement, and Bilateralism.

• *Territorial.* Here the theme is one of establishing independence, and it can develop when companies become too big too fast (through rapid global expansion or a merger or acquisition). Typically, units scattered around the globe seek autonomy from headquarters. They believe that the corporate chiefs are out of touch with local and functional requirements and that the only way they can get the job done or show a profit is as an independent unit. Because excessive autonomy is unacceptable to corporate leaders, games are played to create territories in deed if not in name. The goal is to convince executives that they're adhering to corporate policies and working in concert with larger business strategies, but in fact they are acting on their own. Territorialism can occur on all levels—a country manager operating independently from headquarters or direct reports acting independently from a team leader. An antiauthoritarian, prodecentralization sentiment reigns, and it fosters all sorts of deceptive and manipulative behaviors. As a consequence, the organization starts to operate as a conglomerate of fragmented units. Games frequently played as a function of this DNA include Slush Fund, Sandbagging, Keep Them Guessing, Token Involvement, Marginalize, and Big Splash Career Hopper.

• *Obsessive.* In this case, the theme is one of managing with an insistence that others submit to the leaders' way of doing things. There is an obsessive preoccupation with numbers, trivial details, and showing off. The organization becomes highly analytical, and there is a compulsion to control. Relationships are seen in terms of dominance and submission, and employees perceive the organizational culture as individualistic, cold, and unemotional. The leadership might be seen as unforgiving. Some people will feel detached, which results in a lack of excitement or enthusiasm, indifference to praise or criticism, and a lack of interest in the present or the future. There is a lack of spontaneity and an inability to relax, as these companies want their people competing hard against each other; they see it as analogous to a sports team where those who compete successfully are awarded the starting positions. This DNA stimulates such games as Sandbagging, Quarterly Earnings, Big Splash Career Hopper, Victim, Kill the Messenger, Divide and Conquer, and Scapegoat.

Although other DNAs exist, it's likely that one of these themes is relevant to your company's ecology of games. This doesn't mean that yours is a "bad" company, that it's unsuccessful, or that it's an unpleasant place to work. Mistrust may be in your company's DNA, but the quality control spawned by this mistrust may have also helped you produce high-quality products and avoid the mistakes that plague other companies in your industry. Territorialism may characterize your DNA, but your various de facto independent units may be highly productive and profitable.

The problem is that organizational games DNA places an artificial ceiling on what your company can accomplish. As productive and profitable as your autonomous groups might be, for example, you may be failing to take advantage of economies of scale or synergies that come through interdependence.

To figure out which of the DNA themes applies to your organization, answer the following multiple-choice questions:

1. People at our organization worry the most about which of the following:
   A. That their people are goofing off or not putting much effort or creativity into their work, or that they are incompetent
   B. That they have not been invited to the table for important meetings or decisions
   C. That they are going to have to conform to corporate policies or procedures that they deem ineffective
   D. That they won't perform up to the obsessive expectations and will be viewed as second class
2. When the organization has a bad year or a project fails to meet the high expectations with which it was launched, people usually attribute the problem to:
   A. Other people for making stupid mistakes
   B. Leaders for failing to listen to the people on the line
   C. Organizational insistence that everyone must follow a single strategy, process, or policy
   D. The culture of excessive controls
3. Our CEO's major flaw is:
   A. A propensity to blame others when things go wrong (rather than stepping up and accepting responsibility)
   B. Surrounding himself or herself with an inner circle and not reaching out to others
   C. Failing to acknowledge that different groups in different parts of the organization have different needs and ways of operating
   D. Promoting extreme competition between individuals

4. When our organization achieves a significant success, credit is given to:
   A. An idea or strategy for being right on the mark (rather than to the individuals who executed the idea or strategy)
   B. The individuals who have the best connections
   C. The corporation as a whole
   D. A relatively small number of stars

Clearly, the A answers signify Mistrusting; the B answers, Exclusive; the C answers, Territorial; the D answers, Obsessive.

Knowing which DNA fits your organization is useful, in that it gives you insight into the source of your game ecology. Grasping this ecology is a critical step for any manager who wants to achieve higher levels of performance and creativity. And as we'll see in the next chapter, it's also critical for dealing effectively with organizational change.

CHAPTER 9

The Challenge of Change
Toward a Games-Conscious
Model of Transformation

Business leaders who want to initiate change in their organizations should beware of the games that are being played. In our experience with the organizations for which we have worked and consulted, we've witnessed how games stand in the way of significant change. As Chapter Eight indicated, these games form an ecology that is deep rooted. No matter what a company's tradition, culture, and successes might be, the web of games played by its people constitute a huge inertial force—a force that can resist and potentially sabotage even the best-conceived change efforts. Whether you're a CEO implementing a massive change initiative designed to restructure the organization, or a team leader attempting to institute a new policy, your game ecology can be a serious obstacle.

In *Conquering Organizational Change*, Pierre Mourier and Martin Smith (2001) state that "The professional literature suggests that up to 75 percent of change efforts end in failure" (p. 17). In *The Dance of Change,* Peter Senge and his colleagues (1999) note that "This failure to sustain significant change recurs again and again despite substantial resources committed to the change effort (many are bankrolled by top management), talented and committed people 'driving the change,' and high stakes" (p. 6).

The theories about why change fails are numerous, and they include everything from our natural resistance to change to failure of senior leadership to fund and back the change strategy. We believe, however, that although these and other factors can contribute to the failure of a change initiative, the hidden factor of games is significant. Let's explore how and why this is so.

A Dual Negative Impact

Think about a major change initiative that failed in your organization. The odds are that it was launched with great expectations and energy, but somewhere along the way, it didn't take hold the way everyone thought it would. Perhaps people embraced it initially and made the sought-after changes, but then gradually reverted to traditional behaviors. Or perhaps resistance existed right from the start, with people giving lip service to the change program but sticking to the old ways when the spotlight wasn't on them.

Perhaps those responsible for the change initiative blamed management for not funding the initiative adequately. Or they felt that the support was not sustained—after the initial burst of enthusiasm, management became distracted by other issues. Or the company went through a crisis that took attention and energy away from the change strategy.

More likely, however, no one was quite sure why the change effort failed. The effort seemed to lose steam for no particular reason. With hindsight, there might have been a lot of second-guessing: "If we had done x instead of y, the initiative would have been successful." Ultimately, however, why these things don't work is often a mystery.

We're suggesting that by looking at games and game ecologies, you can shed some light on this mystery. More specifically, consider the primary and secondary effects games have on change efforts.

Primary Effect: Organizational Games DNA Runs Counter to the Essential New Behaviors and Procedures of a Change

As we discussed in Chapter Eight, organizations have a core games theme, a DNA that often revolves around mistrust, exclusivity, territoriality, or obsessiveness (though they may have some other theme). In many ways, DNA defines the culture or "the way things are done around here." It explains a lot of the evolution of processes, procedures, rituals, and games. When a change program calls for new behaviors or procedures that aren't compatible with the DNA, these tend to be rejected.

For instance, let's say an organization's games DNA revolves around exclusivity. Marginalize and Token Involvement are common games, and they produce policies and behaviors in which many people feel left out of decisions and are not included on key teams. Now a new CEO comes in and decides a change is needed, recognizing that the company has rested on its laurels for too long, that competitors have stolen share with cutting-edge products and services, and that people have become complacent. The company is restructured with an eye toward stimulating innovation. In a well-funded, top-down program, the organization is flattened, teams are formed, and policies and procedures are established to encourage knowledge sharing across boundaries. This is a well-thought-out change strategy, and it creates a buzz of excitement and a lot of energy initially. After this buzz diminishes, however, the organizational DNA reasserts itself. Resistance forms against inclusive policies and against participatory decision making. People have been playing Marginalize and Token Involvement all along—they've just been lower key in their playing since the new CEO took over—but these games sabotage many aspects of the change program. They prevent people from fully embracing or trusting policies that encourage them to share information or that promise them they'll be rewarded for innovative ideas. People are so accustomed to behaving in ways that ingratiate themselves with the inner circle or that exclude those who they feel are their rivals that they don't act in ways that are congruent with the company's new goals.

What is so devastating about this games DNA is that it operates below the surface. People don't openly sabotage the new teams or protest the new policies. In many ways, they aren't even conscious that they are sabotaging anything. They are simply acting as their games DNA has programmed them to act. They have been playing games of exclusivity for years, and even though they are being encouraged to adopt new attitudes and behaviors, it's tough to fight against old habits.

Secondary Effect: The Game Ecology Creates Inertia

It may well be that a change effort doesn't run counter to the games DNA in your company. Whatever change you're working toward can be implemented without encountering *direct* resistance from the games being played. We emphasize "direct" because the resistance will still exist, but it will be indirect.

As we've discussed, individual games tend to become reflexes. An ecology of games therefore tends to become a set of interlocking reflexes—in other words, a very rigid and inertial "structure." People automatically behave as games dictate, and a huge infusion of energy (for example, senior leadership attention, resources, and the like) is needed to counteract the inertia. Even if this inertia is overcome temporarily, people can quickly relapse back into old game habits after they've made token behavioral changes and the initial excitement dies down.

Furthermore, games sap organizations of energy, creativity, and adaptability. Any game ecology drains an organization, because people pour a great deal of their time and commitment into the games they play. To play these games well, they need to play them hard. As a result, people can lack the resources and the inclination to embrace change.

Anatomy of a Change: An Example of Games DNA in Action

If you recall Bionic Corporation from our previous chapter, we saw that it is a company where mistrust permeates its DNA and where the game playing feeds this mistrust. David, Bionic's CEO, was not oblivious to the suspiciousness that pervaded his organization. At the same time, he didn't view it from a games perspective.

Of greater concern to David were complaints from customers and some of his staff that Bionic had become too "slow and bureaucratic." The more David investigated these issues, the more alarmed he became, fearing that the company was increasingly vulnerable to competitors. For this reason, at his annual meeting attended by the company's top one hundred leaders, he said the following: "I've been hearing many complaints lately that Bionic is becoming a slow-moving company, and that the complexity of our systems and procedures has grown dramatically over the last few years. In the competitive marketplace in which we're playing, we cannot afford to lose speed. Either we address this issue now or put our company at risk for the future."

With David's talk as the catalyst, Bionic embarked on a change program, designed to simplify the governance structure and controlling reports and to clarify roles and responsibilities. To that end, David appointed a steering committee, designated project leaders for each work stream, and hired a consulting firm to support this change program. David also made sure that everything was fully funded so that he wouldn't hear the all too common excuse, "It would have worked, but we ran out of money."

Two years later, David admitted that the initiative hadn't worked. With hindsight, it was clear that the games DNA was the culprit. That DNA was all about mistrust, so the complex, slow-moving bureaucracy was in place as a monitoring mechanism to prevent people from taking wrongheaded and harmful actions. The games played—Gotcha, Victim, Gray Zone—were all designed to identify mistakes or to help people escape accountability for the "mistakes" that were made.

Viewed in that light, it is no surprise that the games subtly undermined all the positive items on the agenda. For instance, when the controlling reports were simplified, the CFO became anxious. He felt he had lost control of the process and was certain that mistakes would be made. To protect the company and himself, he began scheduling monthly meetings about the reports with each member of his staff, followed by conference calls or online meetings with the top country general managers, during which they went over all the numbers. In this way, the CFO inadvertently restored the complexity and slowness that David wanted to eliminate. Even worse, a number of games emerged around these meetings.

Two years after David started his change program, he admitted that they had removed certain complexities only to replace them with others; that for every process that had been sped up, there was one that had been slowed down. It was incredibly frustrating, as David had the right change strategy in place for the issues facing the company and had put as much financial and leadership support behind it as he could. Unfortunately, David's program ran counter to the company's games DNA, thus demonstrating the primary effect of games on change efforts.

Bionic also illustrates the secondary effect of games—how inertia thwarts change even when the games being played aren't in conflict with the change initiative. About a year after the simplification program failed, Bionic launched a new program to increase top-line revenues. The management team created cross-functional regional teams responsible for identifying opportunities to increase sales. These cross-functional teams were empowered to launch projects designed to capitalize on the best opportunities, and they had solid financial backing to make sure that projects were carried through to the implementation stage. The synergies of different functions working together, combined with the ability to implement programs without having to deal with bureaucratic red tape, did result in some top-line revenue increases for Bionic.

These increases, however, were not as great as expected. In fact, they were rather disappointing. Again, David and his leadership team didn't understand why this change program fell short. In this instance, the games DNA had little direct impact on the program. The pervasive mistrust evidenced in the games didn't conflict in any major way with the cross-functional teams' mandate.

It was only when David and his team sat down with a consultant and reflected on the secondary effect of game playing that they saw how inertia weakened the impact of their program. They realized that the effort given by team members was good but not great. Again with hindsight, David saw that mistrust had generated a strong internal focus, rather than a focus on the market, and an aversion to risk taking, as people wanted to avoid any possibility of failure. Or as one of his leadership team put it, "They handled the assignment competently but not courageously." In other words, no one was willing to explore cutting-edge or breakthrough ideas to increase revenues. They spotlighted opportunities that seemed safe. There was no buzz in the company around these programs, even though they were critical to the company's future. The internal focus and the fear of failure prevented the emergence of the sort of ideas that could have made the difference between good and great.

Overcoming Games DNA and Inertia

Earlier, we discussed the ACE (Awakening, Choice, Execution) method and how individual managers can use it to neutralize games being played in their areas. It would be nice if every manager in the organization would use this method, but organizational leaders can't count on this happening. In fact, they must keep reminding themselves that games die hard, especially during times of change. When unpredictable, confusing, and even scary changes occur, people tend to cling to what's familiar. Anxiety runs high, and games exert an even greater hold on employees when their world is turned upside down by a takeover or in the wake of a downsizing. This is true of people up as well as down the line. If you look around at other top people in your company, you'll find that many individuals who have reached senior levels have done so in part because they're good at playing the particular games the organization favors. As a result, they have a vested interest in these games, and consciously or not, will gravitate to them, especially during times of upheaval. The only exception to this rule occurs when change convinces them that their traditional behaviors, including game-related behaviors, are no longer viable in the new paradigm.

Some companies, anticipating the need for major change and realizing that the organizational games DNA will be a significant barrier and that it is ingrained in the current senior team, will hire a group of senior leaders from outside their organizations to "change the game." The new senior leaders, who understand the importance of games, generally come with a clear mandate. They interrupt the games using one of the approaches proposed in Chapter Seven (for example, calling the games), create an open dialogue with employees, and warn or fire the people who continue playing these games.

These actions disrupt the game ecosystem, but they don't always create the type of environment that helps implement the desired change. Sometimes, they just replace the current organizational games DNA with a new one, thus reproducing the inertia that diminishes the impact of any change strategy.

A much savvier approach was taken by ABC Corporation, a midsize, family-owned high-tech firm that was about to launch a strategy to take the company global. The leadership compared the qualities that would be needed by managers who would be located in satellite offices around the world with the behaviors encouraged by the games DNA. In terms of the qualities required, they determined that managers would require a high degree of independence to be effective; that they would need to make many decisions that corporate headquarters couldn't make; and that being in a given country and understanding its markets, culture, governmental issues, and so on would give these managers greater insight about how to move forward than a senior leader in the United States would have. The willingness of the country managers to think for themselves and not to be a slave to corporate policy and procedures was crucial.

The games DNA, in sharp contrast, revolved around obsessiveness, which resulted in dependence on the CEO and founder of ABC. At ABC, people were not attempting to carve out their own niche and operate free from corporate interference; rather, employees were reluctant to take any action without the approval of the powerful founder of the company. They played Central Approval, the Boss Said, and No Bad News, the first two because of the overwhelming power of the founder, the third because no one wanted to displease him. A fourth game that had become extremely popular was No Decision, because everyone was reluctant to do anything except follow the founder's lead; people routinely tabled discussions on important issues or delayed going forward with programs until the CEO formally issued a directive to move forward.

Fortunately, ABC Corporation conducted a games diagnosis prior to launching its global initiative. The leadership team quickly understood that ABC's game ecology might cause country heads to be overly tied to the mandates of headquarters and that a desire to please the boss might detract from the independence they needed to function effectively. Once the leadership team recognized the inherent conflict between the company's games and its global mission, they began engaging in a deep dialogue about their games DNA. This dialogue included Jonathan, the founder and CEO of the company. Jonathan mentioned in a memorandum to the whole company that he recognized how his behaviors had favored the games (he referred to the games not by name but as routines and attitudes) that existed in the company and that he was personally willing to change. Through this dialogue and through leaders' talking with their direct reports about what had been discussed, the leadership team catalyzed the adoption of the ACE method at various points in the company. Rather quickly, people stopped playing the common organizational games as intensely and as often. They tested new, more independent behaviors in small ways and, when they realized that there were no negative repercussions, were more willing to assert their independence. The ongoing open and honest conversations about games helped keep game playing under control. Even when Jonathan asserted himself or seemed unhappy, this ongoing dialogue helped prevent people from lapsing into their old behaviors.

Though the global initiative is still in the process of being rolled out, the early results look good, and it's clear that most ABC country managers don't reflexively look to corporate before making a decision.

A Games-Conscious Model of Transformation

Before your company embarks on any change effort, your first step, similar to that of ABC Corporation, should be to map out your game ecology and determine your games DNA. The discussion in earlier chapters should help you accomplish this task.

Your second step is to assess the level of challenge you will be facing by comparing your DNA theme with the behaviors and attitudes necessary to make your change effort successful. You can begin by asking yourself the following questions:

Are there games our people play that fly in the face of what we want our change effort to accomplish? Can we identify specific behaviors required for games and how they will decrease the odds of accomplishing change-related goals?

What is the absolutely essential quality or skill that our people must display for us to achieve our change objective? How might our games prevent these people from displaying this quality or using this skill to maximum effect?

Is the impact of our games DNA on our change effort a primary or secondary effect? Does this DNA conflict with our change goals, or is it unlikely to have a direct impact on them?

This last question is absolutely essential. If no direct conflict exists, then you just need to deal with the inertia that arises from game playing, and the ACE model should help you in this regard. Leadership can go through a dialogue to create a change plan, encompassing new structures, processes, and systems that take into account the effects of the current ecology of games.

If, however, you determine that a direct conflict does exist, then you need to engage in deeper discussions about the conflict and possibly work toward "regenerating" your organizational DNA, as discussed in the remaining steps here.

Third, determine if the change effort is worth the cost and if the organization is ready to invest this energy. We're not talking about the financial cost, but the price each individual leader must pay in terms of managing the games she plays and those played by her people. Remember, a company's games are often reflected in the behaviors of its leaders. To make the change happen, these leaders will have to stop engaging in Gray Zone or Bilateralism or any favorite game that they may believe helped them lead effectively. They will need to discourage games their people play, which is likely to result in grumbling, protests, or even resignations. If leadership isn't willing to pay the game-related price, they should not embark on the change effort. Also, consider what is happening in other systems that could impact this organizational change (for example, if regulations are changing in a direction that reinforces the current DNA and thus counters the desired change).

Fourth, if the organization is ready and you are willing to pay the price, move to the process of regenerating your DNA. Regenerating the DNA requires deeper levels of dialogue starting with senior management and then engaging the whole company, so that these individuals will achieve "a state of presence," as described by MIT professor Claus Otto Scharmer (2007) in *Theory U—Leading from the Future as It Emerges*. Leaders will need to rethink and reframe their fundamental assumptions about the organization, including a reflection on their actions (on the games they are playing and why they are playing them), and to generate a new organizational DNA. This happens through exercises in which the leadership team becomes so connected and coherent that they are able to access new future possibilities for the organization in sync with the company's mission, and, from this place, a new DNA can emerge. (Please refer to Scharmer's book for more details about the approach.)

This is a significant step, one not to be taken lightly. Consider that if the organization's DNA for the past thirty years has been one of obsessiveness and dependence on the CEO, made up of limiting beliefs that generated a number of games previously mentioned, then changing it to autonomy and interdependence, affirmative beliefs, means reversing expectations and assumptions up and down the line. To regenerate the DNA in this radical manner requires a significant investment in dialogue and development as well as leaders' modeling new behaviors that reflect the reconceived DNA.

Fifth, communicate a fresh vision for the company; launch strategies that flow from this vision; and create structures, processes, and systems consistent with this new DNA.

Naturally, expect some people to leave the organization during this process. They may be enmeshed in their games and their assumptions to such an extent that they choose to keep them no matter what you say or do. They will drift away and naturally depart.

None of this is easy. At the same time, considering the high failure rate of change initiatives, easy shouldn't matter. If the fate of your organization rests on its ability to make ambitious changes successfully, then you'll accept the challenge of having deep discussions and coming to terms with the games DNA that is holding your company back.

CHAPTER 10

Games at the Top

The Impact of Playing in the Executive Suite

While interviewing various managers and leaders for this book, we often heard words to the effect of, "It's tough to do anything about the games in this company if you're not the CEO. It all starts at the top." At first, we viewed these comments as excuses for not taking action against games; the excuses being a form of the Victim game. Although we still don't believe that this is a completely legitimate excuse— we've seen people make choices to deal effectively with games in their areas even when CEOs aren't behind the effort—we have realized that the CEO and his or her senior management team have the power to influence, originate, diminish, or catalyze game playing in their organizations.

A senior meeting took place in a company that had experienced a major setback related to an environmental problem. The meeting was about what they would release to the press, and, as is often the case, there was a discussion about how to spin the bad news and to avoid taking ownership of the problem. In the midst of the conversation, the head of public relations was proposing a complicated story; she then asked the CEO what he thought. "Why don't we tell it like it was," he suggested. The effect this statement had on the group was galvanizing: the game playing quickly stopped, and an earnest search for good business solutions got under way. The CEO alone has the capacity to stop game playing in its tracks with a few well-chosen words (assuming that the words are backed up by congruent behaviors).

Time after time, we've correlated significant game playing in organizations to CEOs or important senior leaders who indulge in these games themselves. As visible and influential as the CEO is, it was still surprising to us how one individual's behaviors could have such a widespread impact on so many people. More to the point, we were a bit surprised by how game-playing CEOs indirectly encouraged similar behaviors, from the executive suite down to line employees in far-flung satellite offices.

Part of the reason CEOs have this effect is obvious: people throughout an organization reflexively imitate the CEO's behaviors, believing that aping the CEO is both legitimized and a route to success. We also found, however, that game-playing CEOs create an environment that encourages other games that may not be the ones the CEO plays. The CEO communicates through his or her actions that manipulation, hidden agendas, political maneuvering, and passive-aggressive behaviors are all acceptable, even necessary, for survival and success.

Raimondo, for instance, was the CEO of a well-known packaged goods company, and he played the Blame game relentlessly during his short tenure at the top. No doubt, part of the reason he played this game was that the company was hit by a number of negative events shortly after he was brought in from the outside to be CEO. As the company's numbers fell and it received negative publicity, Raimondo blamed the holdover leaders from the previous regime for failing to prepare adequately for the negative events, and fired three of them; he blamed the marketing department for not establishing a strong brand, and reorganized it; and he blamed the company's leading management consulting firm for advising it to pursue a strategy that turned out to be ineffective. Raimondo wasn't completely off base in assigning blame, but the way he did it made it into a game. He was very public in his scapegoating, frequently talking to the media about who was at fault. He never took responsibility for anything that went wrong, always finding a reason why it wasn't his fault.

Although some other managers within Raimondo's organization also indulged in the Blame game, many ended up gravitating toward other games. Ironically, considering all the negative events, one of the most popular was No Bad News. It was as if this game were an antidote to Raimondo's relentless scapegoating. People were so tired of hearing what they or their colleagues were doing wrong, they responded by turning a blind eye to anything negative. They sugarcoated performance reviews, ignored data that weren't positive, and put an optimistic spin on their reports. Of course, these games made a bad organizational situation worse, and the board eventually removed Raimondo from his job.

Our point here is that a CEO can influence game playing in an organization both directly and indirectly. Even if you're not a CEO, you should recognize the impact a top executive has on game-playing frequency and type. At the very least, you may be able to alert your CEO to this problem. Many chief executives aren't even aware that their behaviors constitute a game, and often when you or an executive coach sets them on the path to awareness, they learn to manage these types of behaviors.

Why CEOs Play Games

The first thing we need to examine is why CEOs play games in the first place. The easy answer is that it's human nature to play games. If CEOs rose through the ranks in a game-playing culture or, later in their careers, came to a company where games were widely played, they may simply have adapted to their cultures and adopted certain games. Or they may not play games themselves but countenance them, helping create environments where people feel free to engage in manipulative, win-lose behaviors.

However, CEOs also favor games for a deeper reason: anxiety stemming from great accountability combined with great privilege. Few jobs are more stressful today than being the leader of a large organization. With analysts exerting intense pressure for improved quarterly results, regulatory bodies scrutinizing every move a company makes, disgruntled employees filing lawsuits, and growth strategies taxing the organization's resources, it's not surprising that most CEOs are anxious.

As we've discussed, games reduce anxiety—or at least they do so in the short run. Even the smartest, most accomplished CEOs may believe that no harm is done by playing certain games or allowing others to do so. Games provide the illusion of control, of winning and of achieving certain objectives, and this illusion is especially powerful during times of anxiety. Thinking clearly about games or even seeing them for what they are is challenging when you're under tremendous pressure to improve performance or when one crisis or another is unfolding.

Part of the problem, too, is that the traits most CEOs need to succeed can also draw them into games under times of stress. Most of the senior executives we've talked to have healthy egos, are proud of their abilities and accomplishments, and are politically savvy creatures, alert for both internal and external threats. As Thomas Horton (1992) puts it in *The CEO Paradox*, sometimes it is hard for them to remember that the sun is actually at the center of the solar system and not they. This is where the basic character of the CEO becomes very critical. When operating under high-anxiety conditions, some CEOs can exhibit the following game-friendly characteristics:

- Narcissism
- Hubris
- Paranoia

Let's examine each of these so we can understand how it encourages CEOs to embrace certain types of games.

Narcissism

Most CEOs possess sizable egos. If they didn't, they'd lack the drive necessary to obtain the top spot and the ability to weather the criticism that comes with the job. When that egotism is taken to the next level, however, it results in a narcissistic personality (see Feinberg and Tarrant, 1995, for an excellent summary of the effects of narcissism). Some CEOs have little tolerance for criticism; they need sycophants rather than advisers. They constantly cast themselves in a favorable light, and their actions are often designed to make themselves look good first and the company look good second. Although they may be brilliant strategists or visionaries, their emphasis on appearances can detract from organizational results. More to the point, it can encourage certain types of games.

When CEOs are narcissists, they often play games designed to maintain their sparkling images. Typically this means that they gravitate toward games that make themselves look good while making others look bad. They don't necessarily engage in these games with this goal in mind. Instead, they may simply see their behaviors as a way to maintain their influence, to correct others who make mistakes, and so on. The net effect, however, is to misdirect their own energy toward self-aggrandizement rather than focusing it on the organization itself.

When CEOs play these games, they naturally draw others into them, and it's not surprising that the CEO's direct reports play their own games to preserve the ego of the CEO. They become very clever in hiding any news that might reflect poorly on the CEO and overstating the good news. In these situations, chief executives are often out of touch with the reality of their companies.

Even when the narcissist CEO doesn't play games but simply turns a blind eye to them, his personality encourages others to engage in games in anticipation of the response of his oversized ego. People know that he doesn't want to hear or see anything that might spotlight his mistakes or flaws; they recognize that it's more important to maintain the illusion that he's leading well in the present, even if his actions have negative repercussions in the future.

Consider some of the games that the narcissist CEO plays or engenders:

• *Token Involvement.* The CEO solicits other people's opinions and forms teams to study the problems, but ultimately she ignores what she hears in favor of pursuing her own agenda. She wants the credit for coming up with the ideas and strategies that are successful; allowing others to have a say in key programs or policies might detract from her own image as the company's main idea person and problem solver. Token Involvement allows her to make a show of encouraging a diversity of ideas while maintaining her own high opinion of herself. For example, at the age of sixty-six, Lee Iacocca was still dabbling in the design of cars at Chrysler, overriding the wisdom of engineers and designers, "forcing them to submit long, boxy designs and plenty of chrome, when rounder, cleaner models were clearly winning customers" (Horton, 1992, p. 43).

• *No Bad Feedback.* This one is obvious. The CEO encourages others to provide him with feedback, but sends clear signals that he doesn't want to hear remarks that might prove unflattering. Part of this game involves the CEO's saying something like, "Seleya, let me hear your honest opinion of my new human resources policy," but communicating in other ways that what he really wants is approval. It may be that his body language warns people not to continue into negative territory or that someone who does speak candidly with the CEO becomes persona non grata.

• *Central Approval.* It may be that according to organizational structure and decision-making policies, people don't need the CEO's approval for certain programs or other actions. In reality, however, the CEO expects to be consulted prior to any program launch. In this way, he maintains his highly paternalistic image—people need to ask his permission before doing anything significant.

• *Keep Them Guessing.* Here, the CEO keeps her people on their toes by never communicating her positions clearly—or by communicating one position and then switching to another without acknowledging the switch. This game involves creating uncertainty and causing people to debate what the CEO really believes or intends to do. This feeds the CEO's ego, because everyone is always speculating about her and devoting their time to studying her pronouncements, as if she were a religious figure whose statements require study and interpretation.

• *Kill the Messenger.* This game sends a warning that the CEO doesn't want to hear bad news. The CEO can play this game in innumerable ways: becoming angry at the messenger immediately upon hearing the bad news, talking negatively about the messenger afterwards, or taking action against him. People in the company play this game by sugarcoating negative messages or ignoring them completely. As a consequence, of course, the CEO stops receiving real-time information about the company, which obviously impairs her ability to make good decisions.

Hubris

Hubris is the word Homer used to describe "insolence against the Gods." When you have excessive pride that spills over into arrogance, you're committing the sin of hubris. Some CEOs are particularly vulnerable to hubris, especially when things are going well. In fact, they often think that they can do no wrong. They also tend to feel that no rewards are too great, as they have done a lot "single-handedly," and a lot of the games related to executive pay start here. Their pride is such that they value their own need for accomplishment and approval over the needs of the organization. In some instances, they are too proud to admit that they have made a mistake or that they need another individual's or group's help. Excessive pride does indeed goeth before a fall.

Hubristic leaders can also be narcissistic, but there's an important difference between the two types. Narcissists are primarily concerned with maintaining their image, whereas hubrists are focused on power and achievement; the latter group plays games that flow from their pride in their accomplishments and their position in the world. Perhaps one of the most notorious was John Gutfreund of Salomon brothers. In the opening sequence of *Liar's Poker,* Michael Lewis (1990) describes a massive game of the same name, one that was typical of the behavior Gutfreund himself indulged in the game-playing environment he created in the firm.

Here are some games hubristic CEOs commonly play:

• *Hands Off.* This type of CEO restricts access to files and other types of information. There are also certain duties that only she and she alone can perform. She will tell direct reports that if *x* occurs, they are to do nothing and bring the information directly to her. She will create all sorts of rules and regulations designed to protect what she feels is her territory. The underlying theme of this game is that the CEO is the only one capable of handling key tasks, and she is enormously proud of her ability to do so.

• *Hey Big Spender.* This CEO spends money with a flourish. He relishes public displays of his organization's wealth, and he often involves others in these displays. These games can take the form of throwing lavish dinner parties for the company's top executives, building expensive new headquarters, and criticizing direct reports who fail to live up to a high spending standard.

• *Old War Hero.* This game typically manifests itself when there's debate over a decision. The CEO says words to the effect of, "When we faced this problem five years ago, here's how we solved it." There is a constant harkening back to old triumphs and lessons learned. This CEO frequently draws people into his past to determine the course of the company in the future. He counters objections with such phrases as, "You couldn't know this because you weren't here then." By cloaking himself in past glories, this CEO discourages others from voicing ideas or opinions that are different from his own.

• *World on My Shoulders.* Here, the CEO's game-playing attitude is, "If it weren't for me, everything would fall apart." She frequently involves her people in discussions about how tired she is of dealing with problem x and how no one except her seems to know how to handle a given situation (a difficult customer, a crisis, and so on). A dialogue of complaints forms the basis of this game, and the CEO draws people into the dialogue so that they can express sympathy for this position and gratitude for her presence.

Paranoia

Again, a certain amount of paranoia comes with the CEO territory, and it's not necessarily a bad thing to think that others are out to get you. After all, most CEOs do make some enemies on the way up, and there well may be people out to get them. Being suspicious of competitors and wary of powerful executives who are angling for their jobs or forming alliances with key board members may be a form of self-preservation (see Manfred Kets de Vries, 1994). These attitudes can also help CEOs spot threats to the company before they become dangerous.

Paranoia, however, can turn into fear and cause CEOs to sow distrust and anxiety among their people. The paranoid CEO can become a control freak and micromanage everything that goes on during his watch. Fear drives his game playing, and he often tries to use games to attack his enemies or protect himself from threats, whether real or imagined.

Here are some games that paranoid CEOs play:

• *Gossip.* If a CEO believes that a direct report is angling for her job, she may use this game to spread negative news about this direct report. She may do this subtly but cleverly and win the game by driving the "competitor" from the organization. CEOs also use this game to control people; they may engage people in conversations to communicate that Alyssa will receive a promotion if she continues to meet her objectives and that Sam may not get the plum job he covets if he continues to challenge the CEO's decisions. These games represent indirect communication that causes people to waste time and energy trying to determine who is in and who is on the outs with the CEO.

• *Blame.* Some CEOs fear being identified as the individual responsible for a failure, assuming that the failure label will stick and haunt them for the rest of their careers. Wanting to separate themselves from these failures, they shift responsibility for various mistakes and losses to other parties. The Blame game is not always played overtly; the CEO doesn't simply declare that Rick is responsible for the failure of an acquisition attempt. Instead, he creates a committee to investigate why the acquisition attempt failed, and he influences the information the committee receives and how they arrive at their decision, making sure to communicate in small but significant ways that Rick didn't do everything he might have done.

• *Selective Transparency.* Transparency is in vogue among CEOs, and most leaders today talk about how they're completely open and aboveboard in their communications. The game here is to talk about transparency yet retain hidden agendas. Paranoid CEOs fear being absolutely honest. They worry that others will use their honesty against them. One CEO talked to us about how he was worried about admitting that the prospects for the coming year looked less than stellar and that at least one member of his team would convey his "pessimism" to the board. As a result, this CEO would be cautiously optimistic in his public pronouncements while making plans with a few trusted advisers for a bad year.

• *Persona Non Grata.* Paranoia creates the feeling that "you're either with me or against me." If a paranoid CEO believes someone is talking behind her back or is being disloyal in even minor ways, she may fire this individual, or she'll act as though this person didn't exist. The game here is to foster tremendous fear and uncertainty among the troops in the belief that no one will dare be disloyal for fear of being exiled. CEOs can play this game with a glance (looking at someone as if he were not really there) or a gesture (dismissing what someone says with a wave of the hand). The game can also be played by excluding an executive from a team or failing to consult with him before making decisions that impact his area.

• *What I Want to Hear.* We know a number of CEOs who play this game not only internally but externally—with consultants as well as with employees. They launch teams and other groups with a mandate to think outside the box and to reach a conclusion independent of the conventional wisdom. In fact, these CEOs prejudice the outcomes by stacking team membership in favor of a decision they want or providing such strong direction that it is impossible for the team to reach any conclusion but the one the CEO wants. The paranoid CEO fears that if left to their own devices, these groups would challenge him or go against him with their recommendations. Or he uses these "independent" teams or outside consultants to counter anticipated criticism. The CEO can point to these teams and say, "I pursued this strategy based on the recommendation from Group A."

A More Pragmatic Approach

Knowing senior leaders as we do, we don't expect many of them to stop taking responsibility for everything and remove themselves from the center of crises that seem to pop up daily. For this reason, we'd like to suggest some easy steps any CEO can take to lessen his or her dependence, and organizational dependence, on games.

These recommendations are simply a variation of our earlier ACE model, which helps produce the type of honest, open conversations that cause games to be a less attractive option for most people. They're tailored for CEOs and designed to capitalize on their unique influence on organizational behaviors.

Implementing the following recommendations involves focusing on a key business topic—long-term strategy, top-line growth, budgets, or any other such topic that normally precipitates common organizational games. As long as the CEO knows that in the past, the selected topic often resulted in game playing, then the recommendations should work. What you do about these recommendations depends on your position. If you're a CEO, we encourage you to implement them. If you're a senior leader, we hope you'll talk to your CEO about their benefits to the organization. If you're a manager, we suggest that you share your feelings about game playing with your boss; as part of the discussion, emphasize the role the CEO might play in controlling game playing in your group and the organization as a whole.

• *Host dialogue.* Gather people together around the targeted topic for a meeting or series of meetings. The CEO facilitates the discussion, shows that he needs help to solve this issue, and stays alert for the emergence of games. This means he must monitor his own behaviors for signs of the games he typically plays when this topic is the focus, as well as the games that others initiate. Being games-conscious is critical, and when a game starts to emerge, the CEO must call it—naming the game, explaining why it's counterproductive, and cautioning people against playing it. The goal is to host game-free dialogues about critical topics. In most instances, people come to appreciate these dialogues because they produce much more energy, innovative ideas, and commitment than ones entangled in games.

• *Invite the right people into the dialogue.* The CEO will need to balance the more hardened game players who are nonetheless very knowledgeable about a topic with those more open to dialogue and inquiry. Because they're manipulative and skilled at playing games, the hardened group won't give their games up easily ... or possibly at all.

In addition, CEOs need to invite a diversity of people into the dialogue. It may be that by inviting a variety of viewpoints into a conversation, ingrained game behaviors can be avoided. Introducing external voices into the dialogue—those of customers, analysts, and suppliers—can be particularly effective.

• *Move conversations forward consciously.* As they move the dialogue deeper, CEOs should be highly aware of their own game-triggering behaviors. As they bring conversations to decision points, they are at the greatest risk of doing or saying something that initiates games. This is the time when CEOs' heightened awareness of the games commonly played and how they themselves have catalyzed these games in the past will best serve to thwart game playing in the future.

• *Build processes and structures that are less conducive to game playing.* Specifically, create processes and structures that have

Sufficient simplicity. The simpler things are, the less opportunity there is for manipulation. Complexity is a breeding ground for games. In many cases it is better to design the processes and structures with an aim for 90 percent solutions than to try to design perfect processes and structures that then become baroque. Embrace Occam's razor (the simpler solution is the better one). If a process or organization requires huge amounts of paper to describe it, it hasn't been simplified sufficiently.

Collective design. The more that processes and structures are designed collectively (which we acknowledge is time consuming), the better. Involving people in the design process leaves a lot less room for maneuvering afterwards.

Visible accountability. Whatever performance management systems and reward systems are used, they must reinforce accountability, and people must understand that consequences are systematic (positive and negative). Commitments not met must be followed up. Exceptional performance must be transparently recognized and rewarded.

External orientation. When people are focused on customers, markets, and competitors, they play fewer games. Where the focus is internal, games breed. The CEO can promote an external orientation in subtle ways: in her presentations and themes, in objective-setting processes, in meeting agendas, in her visits to external constituencies, in how organizational structures are set up to deliver to these constituencies, and in how processes are designed to focus on the customer.

Boundary crossing. Processes and structures need to be set up to maximize cross-department cooperation and understanding. As we have seen, a lot of games build up in the crevices that form between departments, such as between finance and commercial. Process design and structural setups should support this cross-functional approach wherever possible.

Assumptions of competence. Processes and systems should be set up on the presumption that people are competent. People will play games to circumvent processes that have been designed on the presumption of incompetence or to "catch" them.

• *Start the movement toward action.* As the dialogue segues into action steps, the potential for game playing increases. The reality that actions are going to be taken may ratchet up the CEO's paranoia. The possibility that a given action will require the CEO to take a stance that may be unpopular may cause the narcissistic CEO to play games. An action step may represent a tacit admission that a previous strategy failed, and the hubristic CEO may start playing games to avoid acknowledging that failure.

As long as CEOs are aware of their game types, they can move their groups toward actionable steps without falling into old game-playing patterns.

A New CEO Responsibility: Maintaining a Low-Game Environment

CEOs should figuratively lock away the company's games in a cabinet in their office. As we've noted, it's impossible to eliminate games; they are part of human nature. But in organizational settings they can be either amplified or minimized, and CEOs should accept a significant responsibility for their role in diminishing the use of games.

In addition, CEOs need to understand and accept accountability for the organizational games DNA and recognize the game ecology that exists. By being aware of the specifics of this DNA and game ecology, they can work with the senior team to ensure that where possible they are not reinforcing it. Awareness goes a long way toward helping CEOs take this responsibility seriously. Throughout this book, we've emphasized the downside of games, how they sap people's energy and minimize their commitment to business goals, cause loss of valuable information, contribute to poor decision making, and so on. The goal of increased productivity thus provides a strong incentive for CEOs to raise their awareness of the games being played throughout their organization as well as the games they themselves play or facilitate.

When chief executives think about games on a regular basis, they put themselves in a much better position to manage the frequency and intensity of game playing. Just moderating their own game-playing tendencies has a profound effect on people throughout the company, sending a clear message that the common games are no longer in favor. The discouraging of games with a few words here and there can have a ripple effect throughout the organization, making everyone aware that the CEO does not countenance this type of behavior.

We're making this organizational transformation sound simple and easy, and we know it's not. Nonetheless, we can't overemphasize that a CEO's actions and words can either promote games or reduce them, and we believe that with sufficient awareness of their negative impact, most CEOs will opt for reducing them. We consider the recommendations outlined in the preceding section to be at the core of effective leadership.

CHAPTER 11

A Sustainable Goal
Transforming Organizations in Small but Significant Ways

We began this book by asking, "Why do people laugh at Dilbert?" We explained that the cartoon portrays many of the games played at work—Token Involvement, Scapegoat, No Bad News, Pseudo Science, Gossip—without naming them as such, and that people laugh because these games are all too familiar. Over the course of the book, we've looked beneath the uneasy laughter—at the fact that all the dissipated energy caused by games is anything but funny.

We've portrayed the downside of games through examples and offered a process that can help any organization or manager mitigate the negative impact of games. What we want to do now is emphasize all the positive effects that accrue to an organization when games are approached properly. To do this, we will describe a company that succeeded in managing its game playing. It's a composite of a number of companies, but it illustrates real benefits that we've observed and how they manifest themselves in different work areas.

The Evolution of Composite Corporation

At Composite Corporation, game playing had spun out of control. Interpersonal games such as Gotcha, Marginalize, and Blame flourished; leaders played Scapegoat and Kill the Messenger. At first, the CEO wasn't particularly aware of these games. Over time, however, he realized that people were spending a lot of time "playing politics and avoiding taking personal responsibility for mistakes." The CEO was worried about how much time and energy these nonproductive games consumed, diminishing the time and energy invested in dealing with the company's business problems and opportunities.

The CEO intuitively recognized that if he could encourage greater transparency and straight talk, game playing would diminish. It took a while for him to get these points across—he did so by modeling the behaviors he advocated and suggesting that other senior executives also model them—but gradually, the game playing receded.

Certain games were so entrenched that it was difficult for people to withdraw from them completely. Gotcha still surfaces more than it should, much to the consternation of the CEO, who hates the finger-pointing inherent in that game. But people no longer play Gotcha and other games at every opportunity and especially when they are under stress. They find other outlets for their anxiety, outlets that usually take the form of honest and open dialogues with peers, direct reports, and bosses. When they worry that they will be blamed for not meeting a deadline or that they can't achieve the stretch goals their groups are given, they broach the subject directly, rather than indirectly through games.

Let's zoom in to examine some of the varied effects of this decrease in game playing.

One of the first positive signs is that relationships are improving. This is occurring both horizontally and vertically as people move away from manipulative and secretive behaviors. Reducing game playing diminishes the distrust and suspicion that are part of any intense gaming atmosphere. At Composite, morale is noticeably improving. Bosses are more willing to be transparent with their direct reports; direct reports are no longer as compelled to hide or spin information when communicating with their supervisors; colleagues are simply more collegial and less likely to view a peer as a rival for a key assignment or promotion. Similarly, relationships with "outsiders"— vendors, consultants, and others—are also improving. People at Composite are much more willing to share information than they had been previously; they are pushing the boundaries of what they share with suppliers, for example.

At the same time, Composite has not become a touchy-feely place where consensus is always achieved. In fact, a high level of productive conflict is occurring as games diminish. People are more willing to challenge each other's assumptions publicly, and vigorous debates ensue. At the same time, this conflict and debate is counterbalanced by better listening—people are starting to really hear what others have to say. Over time, Composite's people are becoming a little less defensive and a little more vulnerable. Fewer "silent participants" attend meetings, increasing the number of debates over ideas but also increasing the quality and quantity of ideas presented.

Information—good news as well as bad—is beginning to flow faster and is ending up in the right people's hands at the right times. Composite's IT system is being redesigned to feed information not just to top management but to the decision makers at all levels. People are becoming less territorial as information becomes more widely available; there is less guarding of turf than in the past.

In meetings, too, the focus at Composite is noticeably shifting away from dog-and-pony shows of slides, huge pre-reads, and carefully rehearsed presentations. In their place, lively debates are taking place as people try to be respectful rather than superficially polite. Instead of nitpicking through the data, people issue fact-based challenges. Employees begin asking more "What if . . . ?" and "Why did you assume that?" questions. There is less dancing around perceived taboo subjects and sacred cows.

Promotions are being made on strengths people possess as well as on key behaviors, such as a demonstrated ability to learn and to change one's mind. Rationales for promotions are becoming much better understood because Composite's performance systems are visible and discussed.

One of the most telling signs of the change at Composite involves watercooler or coffee machine conversations. As games recede into the background, these conversations are less sarcastic about senior management and less likely to involve gossip, rumors, complaints, and backbiting. With greater transparency in a game-reduced environment, people understand the rationale for decisions and have less to gossip or complain about. Indeed, these conversations are more likely to be about customer issues or the next product or the fight with a competitor than about internal politics.

Another subtle but telling shift is occurring at Composite: when people have issues they want to raise, they tend to call or visit with someone rather than precipitate e-mail wars. Straight talk is much more difficult via e-mail than through phone or in-person conversations; Composite's employees are beginning to rely on these more personal forms of communication to deal with substantive issues, reserving e-mail primarily for data or information transmission.

There are remaining areas of bureaucracy at Composite, but these areas are usually open to being challenged through process redesign, rather than being defended by those who benefit from them. People don't just glaze over when others challenge the maddening red tape, as had happened in the past. Just as significantly, people work to meet commitments that they feel they have made to their peers and their teams, not just commitments made with senior management or headquarters.

Performance matters more in the post-game era—not just the pure numbers, although these matter a lot, but understanding the reasons why performance is good or bad. Performance assessments at Composite have become rich dialogues rather than just the communication of a predetermined grade. There is a feeling that assessments are a little more objective and less based on favoritism. Reviews are based on a balanced scorecard, and a healthy balance also exists between the long- and short-term measurement systems.

One of the biggest changes at Composite is how mistakes are handled. Before, Gotcha was played hard and frequently. Although as mentioned, this game still surfaces on occasion, people are much more likely to admit mistakes and share information about them sooner rather than later. People generally aren't beaten up by managers for their mistakes, unless of course they are recurring errors. Instead, the focus is on learning, on prevention, and on being accountable.

Bonus systems at Composite have a higher level of transparency than previously and don't change a lot, nor are they negotiated or manipulated much. Budgets are driven more by external benchmarking, progress versus last year, and healthy debate of assumptions, than by angling to hit an easy bonus target. People are still concerned about bonuses, perks, and raises, but these are no longer the primary drivers of work behaviors. Or rather, people generally trust that if they do a good job, these rewards will come. In addition, because games have faded, informal recognition from management and peers is more frequent and more honest. People are buoyed by this recognition, knowing that it is sincere and indicative that they've performed effectively.

Although Composite experienced some turnover among senior management as the company reduced game playing, many people remain in place, and their attitude has changed. For one thing, they've lost a lot of their former pessimism and cynicism. They really believe that their people can deliver, in part because with less game playing, employees have more time, energy, and commitment. Feedback has become a more important tool for every senior member of the management team—they want and expect to know what they're doing right as well as where they can improve. Intellectual honesty is highly valued. Although the company's leaders still can be egotistical and defensive on occasion, they are much more alert to the negative policies and strategies that result when their egos and defensiveness get in the way of doing what's right.

Five Principles to Keep in Mind

We recognize we've given you a lot to think about as well as to do. No doubt, you may forget some of the ideas we've presented, and in the heat of the business day, you will probably lack the time or inclination to open this book and search for the right approach to deal with a given game.

That's fine. We suspect that just the general lessons of the book—to understand the specific types of games being played, to recognize their negative impact, to substitute open and honest dialogue for games—will serve you well.

What will also serve you well are the following principles; they can guide you in lieu of the more specific, detailed suggestions about how to minimize games:

1. **To game is human.** Your goal is to have fewer and less frequent games, not to eliminate games; some games will be with your company forever.

2. **Games flourish during times of high anxiety.** You can't remove anxiety from your organization, nor should you try; companies need anxiety to fuel performance, and people need to be held accountable for performance, as stressful as that may be. In a game-conscious organization, however, this anxiety and stress are channeled into productive rather than manipulative behaviors.

3. **Your company's games are not comparable to another company's games.** Benchmarking your company against others in terms of game playing is neither important nor useful, particularly because other organizations have different game ecologies.

4. **Minimizing game playing starts at home.** Whether you work in the executive suite or in the mail room, you're prone to playing games. As soon as you deny that you play or facilitate games, you've limited your options for dealing with them. Recognizing this tendency in yourself helps you deal with these issues at a personal level. Only then are you able to address game playing in others.

5. **Dialogue is a natural antidote to games.** Don't embark on a course of "gamocide"—that is, don't create programs and policies to punish game playing. This will serve only to create more games. Speaking openly and honestly discourages game playing.

Don't give up in your quest to achieve greater honesty and intimacy in how people communicate. When it comes to this unfamiliar area of management, we are all amateurs, all learning, all making mistakes. Have faith that despite the errors you may make as you tackle the issues of games, the effort is worth it, especially if you want to increase group and organizational productivity. In the words of the poet Antonio Machado (1997), we wish for great success in the effort to make "sweet honey" from our "old failures."

LIST OF GAMES

This Appendix contains a listing of all the games discussed in this book (as well as a few additional ones), but is by no means exhaustive. We have distilled these games from interviews and discussions, from personal experience, and from examples taken from business literature.

In the following sections we give a brief description of the games we did not discuss in Chapter One; some of them include an example to illustrate the mechanics of how the game is played. If you know of games you'd like to tell us about, further examples of the games we have described, or stories about how games are being interrupted or minimized, we would love to hear from you; you can contact us and send your game to our Web site, www.games-at-work.com.

Interpersonal Games (Played with Peers and Colleagues)

I11. *Hands Off*

The player creates a reputation for himself as someone not to "mess with" on territorial issues—every minor territorial challenge (often in service of a process improvement) is dealt with severely and publicly, warning off others.

Games Described in Chapter One

Interpersonal	Leadership	Budget
Gotcha	Gray Zone	Sandbagging
Marginalize	Keep Them	Slush Fund
Blame	Guessing	Lowballed
The Boss Said	No Decision	Baseline
Big Splash Career	Token	Quarterly
Hopper	Involvement	Earnings
Victim	Kill the	
Gossip	Messenger	
No Bad News	Window Watcher	
Copy	Divide and Conquer	
Pre-Deal	Scapegoat	

Additional Games

Interpersonal	Leadership	Budget
Hands Off	Great Idea	Pseudo Science
Hey Big Spender	Pecking Order	Supply-Date
The Realist	Quality Assurance	Management
Old War Hero	Pre-Alignment	Budget as Firing
Either-Or	Excess	Tool
World on My	Preparation	Saving Sales
Shoulders	Management Only	Premature Sales
Entitlement	by Objectives	Recognition
Persona Non	No Bad Feedback	Channel Stuffing
Grata	Not My Problem	Locked in Brainstorm
Nonavailability	Anymore	

(Continued)

I12. Hey Big Spender

The player manages to spend money on company-paid dinners in exceptional restaurants (above the normal company policy) as well as hotel rooms and other luxuries. She is perceived to be "able to do this" and therefore is seen as somehow protected by senior management, giving her an aura of power that she is able to use to achieve her ends.

Example: Sergei made it a habit to dine in Michelin starred restaurants and stay in penthouse hotel suites. In addition, when he "visited" a site in the United States, instead of coming to the site he would hold court in a hotel room; people needed to travel from the site to visit him. This created an aura that he was somehow well connected because otherwise such expense "abuse" would not be tolerated.

I13. The Realist
When new ideas are brought up, or people express a point of view not in accordance with his, the player simply declares that the ideas are "unrealistic" or presents his own ideas preceded by the word "realistically," thereby giving weight to his own ideas without presenting arguments as to why they are realistic.

I14. Old War Hero
The Old War Hero has seen everything before and therefore knows the potential outcome of every decision. This game involves assuming the mantle of the grizzled veteran, and because this person has been through the wars, his views are not subject to challenge.

Example: When discussing a potential new approach to a labor relations dispute, which involved a bit of a gamble regarding employee bonus payouts, a junior HR manager was told by the senior HR manager that "We tried that in '76 and it backfired." When the junior HR manager tried to get more details to determine whether the situation was analogous or not, the details were skimmed over with the clear view that the approach would backfire again.

I15. Either-Or

The player presents a decision to be made as being between two alternatives, one of which is "weak," the other being the one she supports. By making it appear to be a binary choice, the player persuades people to go with her argument, but omits the third or any other possibilities.

Example: In a presentation on organizational design in a chemical company, the presenter sets up two alternative structures: a country-based structure or a global business unit structure. The proposal of the country-based structure was one of extreme autonomy, and this was set up to be shot down (lack of synergy and global standards, and so on) so that the only other alternative presented (which was an extreme global business unit structure) would be the hands-down choice.

I16. World on My Shoulders

The player always looks weary (and continuously mentions the hours of personal time he dedicates), and also states frequently that if it weren't for him, x, y, or z calamity would occur, because he is actually holding things together. (He is unrecognized for this, of course, and others undeservingly get recognition.) This wins some sympathy and convinces some people of the essential contribution the player makes. The game is about winning sympathy and avoiding criticism. (Who would kick someone while he's down?)

I17. Entitlement

The player believes she is entitled to immunity (or a special severance package) for having worked for the company or having been a friend to the CEO for many years, despite the fact that she was already duly compensated. The Entitlement game requires players to gain preference or privilege because of "equity earned" rather than real contributions in the present or in the future.

Example: A regional manager who had not been able to effectively make the transition from country manager to regional manager expected special treatment because of how he had performed as a country manager—instead of focusing on what he could do to become a better regional manager. This constant reference to the past and to his connections in the past was designed to draw the focus away from not only his shortcomings as a regional manager but also his lack of interest in trying to improve.

I18. Persona Non Grata

This game is about ostracizing individuals, often for trivial or vindictive reasons.

Example: A senior commercial manager resigned. He had been the proposed successor to the CEO position, but as soon as it was clear that he was no longer a "player" in the company, criticism of his management style began. In addition, the CEO took the decision badly, and he started to drop subtle hints that the manager lacked the right stuff for succession anyway.

I19. Nonavailability

In this game, the player is able to influence things in her favor by managing agendas so that she is always unavailable to the people who have a different perspective. People win this game when they don't have to take other perspectives into account because they successfully avoided those individuals who might voice such perspectives.

Example: A passionate country manager of Italy had a radical idea with regard to where he wanted to take the Italian business; however, it would require a serious reorganization, the firing of some key people, and some financial support. The regional head did not want to have to say no to the proposal (if he did so, it would be difficult to hold the country manager accountable), but somehow was never available long enough to finish the conversation, and by the time the budget cycle came around, nothing was decided, and no one ever addressed the radical idea.

I20. Stealing Credit

In this game, the player takes credit, in subtle or less subtle ways, for work he didn't do, by either repackaging it, putting his name on slides, or being so effusive in his praise of the idea generator that he's seen as someone who must deserve some praise. (Why else would he be so effusive?)

Example: Minoru once "rediscovered" her own slides in a presentation that was being made to a steering committee for the redesign of a pension plan. The slides were listed under another person's name, were in a new format, and made no reference to Minoru's work, but they were almost completely unchanged.

I21. Home-Field Advantage

By making people come to her territory or room for a meeting, the player exercises subtle power over the meeting process (in terms of the arrangement of chairs, surprise invitations to others, the length of time of the meeting, the player's availability at the start of the meeting, and so on).

Example: This has always been an important issue in diplomatic meetings, and to some extent in certain important business settings. It can be a complex task just to seat diplomatic delegations. According to Dr. U Maung Gyi, professor of law and linguistics at Ohio University, "It took a year for the United

States and North Vietnam to agree on the shape and size of the table at the Paris peace talks." In contrast, Gyi noted, setting up a diplomatic meeting room can be relatively easy if the VIPs desire cooperation, as President Reagan and Soviet Premier Mikhail Gorbachev did in their 1986 meeting in Reykjavik, Iceland. They sat at a simple, square table and placed the interpreters on the sides "as significant partners in the negotiation process."

122. Public Challenge of Your Loyalty

In this game, the player publicly challenges a person's loyalty to the organization or a change effort, just because that person has raised some legitimate concerns with the way the organization is approaching an issue, rather than responding to the concerns.

Example: Probably the classic example of this was in Maoist China. As Mao wrote in his *Red Book,* "In the ideological field, the question of who will win in the struggle between the proletariat and the bourgeoisie has not been really settled yet. We still have to wage a protracted struggle against bourgeois and petty-bourgeois ideology. It is wrong not to understand this and to give up ideological struggle. All erroneous ideas, all poisonous weeds, all ghosts and monsters, must be subjected to criticism; in no circumstance should they be allowed to spread unchecked."

123. Pampering a VIP

In this game, extraordinary efforts are devoted to hosting the senior manager—nothing is too much—so that the manager leaves with a positive impression and, because certain personal wishes have been fulfilled (to do with comfort or entertainment), will find it difficult to challenge business results.

124. Smoke-Filled Rooms

In this game, meetings are mere formalities, and real decisions are made in hallways and other out-of-the-way meeting places. It's all about isolating the decision maker and getting a decision made before the formal process begins. Members of the team who were not there are surprised, and have lost their influence.

125. Half-Truths

The player states only half of what would be necessary for others to know. As a result, people make decisions as if half-truths were whole truths. In this game, people pretend not to know all the facts so that if they're later accused of misleading the group, they can claim ignorance.

126. Deliberate Leak

In this game, a document is deliberately leaked (either internally or externally) in order to discredit someone.

Example: An employee had been asked by his boss for a summary of a recent meeting. Expecting that the summary would be kept confidential, the employee wrote a report, including his assessment of the positions each of the different meeting members took. While this employee was on vacation, his report was sent directly to all the meeting participants, with a cover letter describing the high levels of "transparency" that were being sought.

127. Bcc

When sending an e-mail, the player sends a blind copy to another recipient so that the original recipient doesn't know that the player has copied someone else. Some of the common purposes for playing Bcc are to let other people know that you have taken action, to show that you are really strong in representing a particular point of view to a third party, or to block the possibility that someone can say later that he was not informed.

Leadership Games (Played with Subordinates or Consultants)

L9. Great Idea

The player recognizes his direct report (or someone else) in front of a group for a good idea, subtly establishing hierarchy. (Only a higher-level executive would recognize another professional's idea in public.)

L10. Pecking Order

In this game, people play favorites and put others in the doghouse as an exercise of power. The game is to establish a hierarchy of sorts, an informal ranking of players in a given group.

L11. Quality Assurance

The player calls the client to check whether her direct report has done what she was supposed to do. Her direct report, however, doesn't realize that the player is doing this. Through this game, the player makes sure that it is clear to the client who the boss is.

L12. Pre-Alignment

In a meeting, a direct report presents some ideas that she had not discussed in advance with her boss. Her boss immediately kills the proposal, whether or not it would be a good idea. This can be contrasted with the game Pre-Deal (see Chapter One) in that the lack of a pre-deal dooms the idea.

L13. Excess Preparation

The player prepares a presentation to the executive team with 5 slides and 140 backups. He has answers to any possible question they ask. The game here is never to be caught without an answer to a question, the assumption being that preparation is all that counts.

L14. Management Only by Objectives

In this game, a company installs a strong meritocracy based on MBO. A good year-end rating will result in a high bonus and good career; a low year-end rating will result in poor career progression. What makes this a game is that the manager does not take into account any other factors in assessing performance (such as major uncontrollable external events or a change of plans midyear), and this creates a climate where people feel very much hostages to fortune, or where people compete unfairly to win at all costs. This game is particularly insidious because it operates behind a guise of objectivity; it allows players to justify their decisions about promotions, bonuses, and salary increases as "perfectly logical" when those decisions are only logical from a very narrow perspective.

L15. No Bad Feedback

In this game, the boss avoids giving negative feedback to the employee because she doesn't want to hurt the employee's feelings. This game is often played in companies with "civilized" cultures where straight talk is often absent. People feel that certain individuals can't take bad feedback or that it's better to keep others in the dark than to confront them with harsh realities.

L16. Not My Problem Anymore

Just before retiring from the company, an executive gives overly generous salary increases to all his direct reports. (Variation: A boss promotes a low performer to another team to get rid of her.)

L17. Let's Not Rock the Boat

In this game, a manager systematically kills ideas through phrases that sound like "Let's not rock the boat." This is intended to mean that the idea being proposed is likely to have a destabilizing effect or to challenge his superiors with its revolutionary nature. However, this is just a front for a manager who wants to preserve the status quo.

L18. Central Approval

This is a power game, pure and simple. Leaders playing Central Approval require that certain or all decisions must be approved by them. It's not that they particularly want to make those decisions, but rather that they want to communicate to everyone that they are in charge. Often played with headcounts and travel expenses.

L19. Hide Behind Written Documents

This is a paperwork game, one where any problems or concerns are answered by detailed, official documents. The game is to use paperwork to justify actions and defend bad decisions.

L20. Selective Transparency

In this game, the player is perfectly willing to require other senior people to reveal personal information, but refuses to make such information available herself.

L21. *Vague Big Vision*

In this game, the senior leader sets out a big vision ("creating a flexible organization," for example) that is so vague that any plan and program he launches can fit into it, but is also vague enough that he'll never be held accountable for it.

L22. *Show Up Differently*

In this game, the player deliberately shows up at work in different moods (angry, upset, calm, rational, impulsive, and so on) to keep her people on their toes. She uses these mood swings to manipulate her staff. People pay attention to the player because her moods are so volatile, making her more intimidating.

L23. *Soothing Guilt*

In this game, a person does something nice to make amends for doing something wrong (or failing to take appropriate action earlier). For example, a manager who feels guilty for firing a poor performer without having given the employee appropriate feedback might then give the employee a generous severance package to soothe his conscience. The game is that the nice action is not the appropriate response to the error.

L24. *Bilateralism*

In this game, the player never brings important business topics to her management team meetings. She prefers to manage critical decisions bilaterally with her subordinates, therefore preventing a team's forming, which allows her greater control. When confronted with this behavior, the player might explain that her decision-making process accelerated decisions in the company. However, using this approach, the player misses out on the power of dialogue and its impact on the quality of the decision.

L25. Nepotism
This game entails inserting children or relatives of senior management into selection processes and exercising pressure (usually subtle) to have them hired.

L26. Glossing Over
When confronted with a fact or data point that would require a leader to change course, strategy, or a decision in a way that he doesn't want to, he "glosses over it." This game can be played in a hundred different ways, but it often involves finding a way to dismiss a key piece of information; the player might question its source or suggest that it's not valid in this particular circumstance. The real issue, though, is that the player doesn't want to deal with the information, so he deliberately reduces its importance.

L27. Populist
In this game, the player creates good rapport with many levels of subordinates through town hall meetings and other devices. During these meetings, the player sends very positive messages, but her actions often have a negative impact in the long run. Still, these efforts increase her popularity and make it seem as if she has the best interests of the whole at heart, often putting her direct reports in a tough spot.

L28. Overstrict Policies
The game here is to intimidate and control through micromanagement. These policies create fear, even though everyone

violates them on occasion because they're absurdly rigid. This game is played by Big Brother–minded leaders.

L29. Renamed Project
In this game, the player hires a consultant under the approval of one project but then asks the consultant to do another (unauthorized) project under that purchase order.

L30. Rubber-Stamp
In this game, the player hires a consultant to do a feasibility study of a project she already knows is feasible; she needs an external person to deem the project "worthy" so that senior management will approve it.

Example: At a company that had recently been bought by another company in a slightly different sector, a senior manager in the acquired company identified which consulting group the acquirer typically used, and briefed this consulting group on his proposed reorganization of the unit. The consulting company then prepared the "data" and arguments to support this position, and ultimately the proposal was approved because the consulting company was credible to senior management and had "stamped" the proposal. The added advantage for the manager was a diminution of responsibility for the proposal; if the idea failed, the manager could move to play Scapegoat.

L31. Spies
In this game, consultants are sent in with an official mandate to help with an organizational problem, but with a real mandate to report back on individuals.

L32. Outsourcing Management to Consultants

In this game, a manager outsources her main responsibilities (or her people's responsibilities) to a consultant. This happens especially in the areas of strategy, decision making, and talent management. Central to this game is the outsourcing of key tasks while you retain the position and pay for your position.

Example: Fletcher, the CEO of a multibillion-dollar pharmaceutical company, didn't trust the competence of his people for making important decisions. He preferred to hire a few of his trusted consultants for such subjects as defining their regional strategies or hiring a senior executive. His direct reports accommodated to this game and also started engaging consultants for their critical tasks.

L33. What I Want to Hear

In this game, a manager launches a team or teams to come up with recommended solutions to a problem. (This can be played with internal teams or with consultants.) Teams are often launched with an objective to really "think outside the box." However, the manager has a twofold agenda: to get an answer that he has predetermined as the best solution and to make it seem as though this solution came from these "independent" teams. The manager achieves this either by stacking the team with some confidants who have been given the mission explicitly, or alternatively by skillfully using meetings to steer the group or groups to the "correct" answer. This game helps fend off any later criticism of the decision (and possibly pave the way to some scapegoating if it doesn't work out well). What I Want to Hear is in some senses an elaborate and highly structured version of Token Involvement.

Budget Games

B5. Pseudo Science

In this game, the player uses highly specific and often meaningless ratios and statistics to justify a decision. The proposal is given a kind of "sanctity" by the use of the numbers and ratios and benchmarks; this often renders the decision undiscussable in certain forums, and shifts attention to specific aspects of the issue that may not be the most important, but that support the player's particular agenda.

B6. Supply-Date Management

In this game, internal customers ask for supply (for example, of a project or report) earlier than they really need it because they don't trust that it will be delivered on time. Suppliers know this and therefore don't deliver by the date requested.

B7. Budget as Firing Tool

The boss is uncomfortable firing a subordinate and therefore sets an "impossible" budget that will give him this leverage, as there is no way the subordinate can achieve his goals with the severe financial constraints.

B8(a). Saving Sales

In this game, the players save sales for next year when this year's budget is already met.

B8(b). Premature Sales Recognition

In this game, which is the opposite of Saving Sales, players record a highly contingent sale as a way to pad sales figures.

Example: Web software developer MicroStrategy rode a wave of seemingly galloping revenue growth under CEO Michael Saylor. However, it turned out that sales for 1998 and 1999 were overstated. When software was sold, the company booked not just the sale of the software but also hypothetical sales of future upgrades. A $12.6 million profit was changed to a $34 million loss when restated, and the stock lost 62 percent of its value in a single day. The SEC filed suits, and employees were laid off.

B9. Channel Stuffing

To meet or exceed this year's budget, players create sales by stuffing the channels when the customers have not really bought the product.

Example: While CEO of Sunbeam, Al Dunlap used channel stuffing to support earnings gains. He sold millions of dollars' worth of backyard grills to customers like Sears and Wal-Mart in the middle of winter, though the grills would not hit sales floors until spring or summer. Grills stayed in warehouses, allowed deferred payment, and allowed returns of unsold merchandise. The company really was just moving the grills off-site. Eventually the company filed for bankruptcy.

B10. Locked in Brainstorm

In this game, people are asked to propose a "blue sky" budget in the spirit of brainstorming and then find that the budget has already been locked in by finance. The game is therefore all about pretending to give people freedom to request the funds they need to accomplish stretch goals.

REFERENCES

Berne, E. *What Do You Say After You Say Hello?* New York: Bantam Books, 1972.

Berne, E. *Games People Play: The Basic Handbook of Transactional Analysis.* New York: Ballantine Books, 1996.

Cashman, K. *Leadership from the Inside Out: Becoming a Leader for Life.* San Francisco: Berrett-Koehler, 2008.

Collingwood, H. "The Earnings Game: Everyone Plays, Nobody Wins." *Harvard Business Review,* June 2001, pp. 65–74.

Collins, J. "Level 5 Leadership: The Triumph of Humility and Fierce Resolve." *Harvard Business Review,* July 2005, pp. 136–146.

Fienberg, M., and Tarrant, J. *Why Smart People Do Dumb Things: Lessons from the New Science of Behavioral Economics.* New York: Fireside, 1995.

Hope, J., and Fraser, R. *Beyond Budgeting: How Managers Can Break Free from the Annual Performance Trap.* Boston: Harvard Business School Press, 2003.

Horton, T. *The CEO Paradox: The Privilege and Accountability of Leadership.* New York: AMACOM, 1992.

Kets de Vries, M. *Organizational Paradoxes.* Boston: Cengage Learning, 1994.

Lewin, K. "Force Field Analysis: Understanding the Pressures for and Against Change." www.mindtools.com/pages/article/new TED_06.htm, n.d. (accessed Oct. 24, 2008).

Lewis, M. *Liar's Poker: Rising Through the Wreckage on Wall Street.* Harmondsworth, England: Penguin Books, 1990.

Machado, A. *Poesias Completas.* Madrid: Espasa Calpe, 1997.

Maslow, A. *Motivation and Personality*. New York: HarperCollins, 1987.

McClelland, D. *Human Motivation*. Cambridge: Cambridge University Press, 1988.

Mourier, P., and Smith, M. *Conquering Organizational Change: How to Succeed Where Most Companies Fail*. Atlanta, Ga.: CEP Press, 2001.

Neumann, J. von, and Morgenstern, O. *Theory of Games and Economic Behaviour*. (60th anniversary ed.) Princeton, N.J.: Princeton University Press, 2007. (Originally published 1944.)

Oliver, M. "The Journey." *Dream Work*. New York: Atlantic Monthly Press, 1994.

Scharmer, C. O. *Theory U—Leading from the Future as It Emerges*. Cambridge, Mass.: Society for Organizational Learning, 2007.

Semler, R. *Maverick: The Success Story Behind the World's Most Unusual Workplace*. Boston: Grand Central Publishing, 1995.

Senge, P. M., Kleiner, A., Roberts, C., and Ross, R. *The Fifth Discipline Fieldbook*. New York: Doubleday, 1984.

Senge, P. M., and others. *The Dance of Change: The Challenges to Sustaining Momentum in Learning Organizations*. New York: Doubleday, 1999.

Tse-tung, M. *Quotations from Mao Tse-tung: The Little Red Book*. Beijing: Peking Foreign Language Press, 1970.

Whyte, D. *Crossing the Unknown Sea*. New York: Riverhead Trade, 2002.

ACKNOWLEDGMENTS

Writing a book is always an intense and transformative process. You start with a good idea in mind and the knowledge you bring from your past, and you are transformed through research, many interesting conversations, and the writing process itself. We take this opportunity to thank all those who supported us on this path.

Thanks go to our friends and colleagues who were kind in providing us, in formal and informal conversations with stories and examples from their own professional experience. In particular, a big thank-you to Andreas Struengmann, Andrew Oakley, Arri Pauw, Bill McCarthy, Corey Seitz, Eric Poll, Kevin Cashman, Mauricio Adade, Nelson Libbos, Ney Silva, and Thomas Struengmann for the interviews they gave us.

Our clients, customers, bosses, networks, teams, and CEOs offered us a platform we needed to go deeper and test many of the ideas and concepts in this book in different organizations, industries, and geographies. They provided us with live examples of games and of how to reduce them, and confirmed to us that what we were describing was a real and vital issue for business. Special thanks for their patience and belief in our capacity to support them through important changes.

Our thinking was inspired by a number of authors, teachers, mentors, leaders, and healers who touched our existence.

To name a few, we are thankful to Artur Tacla, Barbara Ann Brennan, Bert Hellinger, Chris Argyris, Claus Otto Scharmer, David Whyte, Eric Berne, Kevin Cashman, Peter Block, Thomas Gross, and Vaclav Havel for their insight and ideas that either indirectly influenced us or appear in some way and form through this book.

Thanks to Rebecca Browning, Genoveva Llosa, Erin Moy, Gayle Mak, Michele Jones, Sophia Seidner, and Mary Garrett from Jossey-Bass for their editorial gifts and advice, and to Bruce for his support and ideas during the whole process.

Our parents and, through them, all our ancestors have paved the path for what we know and do now. Now our own children expose and challenge our own games. We are deeply thankful to them for all the learning they offer us, and we hope that our book and ideas can serve to make the organizations they may work in someday more human and intimate places.

Finally, our warmest thank-you to our wives (Larissa and Diane) for their immense love, patience, and support during the considerable amount of time we were out studying, reading, thinking, talking, and writing.

The points of view and, of course, any mistakes in this book remain our responsibility, and are in no way a reflection on current or previous organizations or employers we have had the privilege to serve.

Mauricio Goldstein is the founder of Pulsus Consulting Group, a consulting company focused on organizational transformation, including such projects as globalizations, mergers and acquisitions, business model redefinitions, organization redesigns, and culture changes. His life task is to partner with and coach leaders in their companies' transformation process to create value and achieve sustainable, superior performance, while unleashing passion and potential. He has consulted to a number of Fortune 500 companies, such as AstraZeneca, Cargill, Intervet, Itaú, Natura, Johnson & Johnson, Nestlé, Novartis, PepsiCo, Sodexo, and Schering-Plough, in Latin America, North America, Europe, and Africa.

Over the years, Mauricio has received a number of awards for business impact, innovation, and academic performance from global corporations and public institutions and has published articles on a variety of subjects, from consumer behavior to knowledge management and culture change. He holds a BSc in industrial engineering (1990) and an MSc in consumer behavior (1996) from the University of São Paulo (Brazil), a diploma in Brennan Healing Science (2003) from the Barbara Brennan School of Healing, and an advanced certificate in organization development and human resources management (2004) from Columbia University.

Mauricio currently lives in São Paulo, Brazil, with his wife, Larissa, and their two boys, Yoram and Benny.

Philip Read has worked in a number of senior roles in human resources for Fortune 100 companies over the last twenty-two years. He has lived and worked in the United Kingdom, the United States, China, Switzerland, Germany, and Spain, and has done business in sixty-four countries around the world. He has won a number of awards for his work, including the PricewaterhouseCoopers and Linkage, Inc. "Most Innovative HR Department" award as part of the global HR leadership team of Dow Chemical, and was selected as one of the international executives whose career was studied for the book *Developing Global Executives,* by Morgan W. McCall Jr. and George P. Hollenbeck.

Over the years, Phil has led large restructuring projects, projects to drive rapid business growth in emerging markets, and projects to form significant joint ventures and integrate major acquisitions. He holds master's degrees in natural science from Cambridge University and in international policy from the University of Bristol.

A native of Scotland, Phil has won the Open Essay prize at Corpus Christi College, Cambridge, the Open String Solo prize at the Edinburgh Music Festival for his cello playing, and has completed a number of mountain marathons including the grueling forty-nine-mile Davos Alpine marathon. He currently lives in Switzerland with his wife, Diane, and their two children, Danny and Natasha.

INDEX

A

Acceptance, reaching, and moving forward, 106–107

Accountability, 194, 196

ACE method: described, 95–96; using, to overcome games DNA and inertia, 171–175, 176; variation of the, to address executive game playing, 192–196. *See also* Awakening; Choice; Execution

Achievement need, 87

Action steps, movement toward, starting the, 195–196

Adams, S., 4, 5

Affiliation need, 85

Alternative solutions, finding, 142

Anxiety: and change, 172; and executive game playing, 182–183, 189; and interrupting a game, 136, 138; issue of, and choosing not to play, 108, 109–110, 114, 119; and organizational environment, 10; and pervasiveness of games, 65, 66; principle involving, 204

Anxiety-reducing dialogue, facilitating, 138–146

Assumptions: challenging, 94, 200; rethinking and reframing, 177

Attention need, 69

Authenticity and courage, 122–124

Awakening: within the ACE method, 96; defined, 95; described, 96–107

Awareness: assessing, 91; heightened, by executives, 193–194, 196, 197; importance of, and understanding of games, 7, 11; intellectual, moving from, to emotional awareness, 103; lack of, as a reason for not confronting games, 84; levels of, range in, 42–45. *See also* Awakening

B

Bcc game, 214–215

Belonging needs, 109

Benchmarking, issue with, 204

Berne, E., 6, 12, 128

Beyond Budgeting (Hope and Fraser), 56

Big Splash Career Hopper game, 23–24, 55, 61, 69, 77, 143–144, 160, 161

Bilateralism game, 159, 176, 218–219

Blame game: choosing not to play the, 115; described, 22; and executive game playing, 180–181,

the, 136–138; not confronting the, reasons for, 87; pervasiveness of, reasons for the, 67, 70

Costa, J. D., xi

Counterproductive games: defined, 15; humor derived from, example of, 4–5

Courage: authenticity and, 122–124; feeling good about having, 136

Cross Up step, the: charting, 134; described, 128; example of, 130; interrupting at, identifying options for, 134

Cross-functional approach, supporting, 195

Culture. *See* Organizational culture

D

Dance of Change, The (Senge and others), 165

Decision making: about whether or not to play games, process for, 110–112; impact of games on, 55–56

Deliberate Leak game, 86, 214

Denial, 17, 104

Diagnosis of games, 154–156, 174

Dialogue, open and ongoing: evolution of an organization reflecting, 199–202; as a natural antidote to games, 205; steps toward, 138–146, 192–194

Dialogue skills, 141–142

Dilbert cartoon, 4, 5, 198

Dirty little corporate secret, 51–53

Distrustful atmosphere: diminishing, 200; effect of a, 73–74, 157–158; and executive game playing, 189. *See also* Mistrusting DNA

Diversion need, 69–70

Diversity, inviting, into dialogue, 193

Divide and Conquer game, 38, 115, 161

DNA of games. *See* Organizational games DNA

Dunlap, A., 223

E

Ecology of games. *See* Game ecology

Egotism becoming narcissism, 183–186

Either-Or game, 56, 210

Emotional and intellectual process: awareness as an, 102–106; choice as an, 118–122

Emotions and feelings, coming to terms with, 145–146

Entitlement game, 59, 210–211

Environment. *See* Organizational environment

Esteem needs, 109

Excess Preparation game, 55, 216

Excessive game playing, result of, 52, 63

Exclusive DNA, 159, 163, 166–167

Execution: within the ACE method, 96; defined, 96; described, 125–146

Executive game playing, 179–197

Exit choice, 114

External and internal factors: assessing the impact of, 79–82; promoting a game-playing environment, 70–77, 147

External focus vs. internal focus, 53, 195

Externally oriented assessment, 62–63

F

Facts, focusing on, 139–140, 141
Fear: assessing, 93; and executive game playing, 191; paranoia turning into, 189, 190; presence of, in making a choice, 122; as a reason for not confronting games, 88–90, 145
Feedback: and game consciousness, 43; game playing involving, 12–14; on interrupting a game, 135–136; receiving a wake-up call through, 104–105. *See also* No Bad Feedback game
Feelings and emotions, coming to terms with, 145–146
Fienberg, M., 183
Fifth Discipline Fieldbook, The (Senge, Kleiner, Roberts, and Ross), 152
Force field analysis, 126–127
Ford Motor Co., Grimshaw v., 88
Fraser, R., 56

G

Game consciousness, range in, 42–45, 97
Game damage, 4, 5, 6, 14, 46–64
Game DNA. *See* Organizational games DNA
Game ecology: defined, 1, 148; example of, *151*; executives recognizing and accepting responsibility for, 196; identifying, 152–153; inertia created by, 167–168; interconnections of, described, 147–163; reflexes in, 168; role of, in not confronting games, 90; and the trance-like state, 104

Game sequence: steps in the, 128–132; writing the, 133–134
Game theory, elements of, 12
Games: additional, list of, *207–208*; budget, 39–42, 222–223; frequently played, list of, *20*, *207*; history of, 65; insidiousness of, 46, 49; interpersonal, 19–31, 206, 209–215; leadership, 31–39, 215–221; odds of reducing, 7; perception of, 51–53; purpose of, 65; responses to, variation in, 1; theory and practice of, 12–14. *See also specific games and aspects of games*
Games diagnosis, 154–156, 174
Games People Play (Berne), 12
"Gamocide," 205
Gavin, B., 121
Gimmick step, the: charting, 133; described, 128; example of, 129; interrupting at, identifying options for, 134; refusing to initiate, 131
Glossing Over game, 219
Goleman, D., xii
Gorbachev, M., 213
Gossip game: described, 27–28; and the Dilbert cartoon, 198; and executive game playing, 189–190; and game ecology, 149, 151, 152; impact of the, 50, 58–59; interrupting the, 132; pervasiveness of, reasons for the, 68–69, 70, 73, 77
Gotcha game: and awakening, 103; and the challenge of change, 169; described, 14, 19–21; and game consciousness, 43; and game ecology, 149, 150, 151, 152, 157–158, 159; impact of the, 47–48, 50, 58, 60; interrupting

the, 132; not confronting
the, reasons for, 86; and
organizational evolution, 202;
pervasiveness of, reasons for
the, 68–69; transforming a
company to diminish the, 199
Gray Zone game: and the
challenge of change, 169, 176;
choosing not to play the, 115;
described, 31–32; and game
ecology, 149, 150, *151*, 157, 159;
impact of the, 53, 61; not
confronting the, reasons for,
84; pervasiveness of, reasons
for the, 70, 74, 78
Great Idea game, 55–56, 60, 215
Grimshaw v. *Ford Motor Co.*, 88
Group activity, as a game-playing
trait, 17
Gutfreund, J., 187
Gyi, U. M., 212–213

H

Habits, 16, *96*, 97, 167, 168
Half-Truths game, 86, 214
Hands Off game, 61, 187–188, 206
Haves and have-nots, gaps between
the, effect of, 75–76
Helping forces, increasing, while
reducing hindering forces,
126–127
Helplessness, sense of, 6
Hey Big Spender game, 188, 208–209
Hide Behind Written Documents
game, 217
Hierarchical structures, effect of,
75–76
Hierarchy of needs, 109
Hindering forces, reducing, while
increasing helping forces,
126–127

History: of game ecology
evolution, creating a, 155;
of games, 65
Home-Field Advantage game,
212–213
Homer, 187
Honesty, fear of, 190
Hope, J., 56
Horton, T., 183, 185
Host dialogue, 193
Hubris, 187–189
Human Motivation (McClelland),
84–85
Human nature, game playing as
part of, 1, 6, 84, 204

I

Iacocca, L., 185
Identity issues, 123, 140, 141
Illusion of control, 183, 185
Individually based work, likelihood
of game playing during, 18
Inertia: described, 167–168; example
of, 170–171; overcoming, 171–175
Innovation, impact of games on,
50–51
Intellectual and emotional process:
awareness as an, 102–106; choice
as an, 118–122
Internal and external factors:
assessing the impact of, 79–82;
promoting a game-playing
environment, 70–77, 147
Internal focus vs. external focus,
53, 195
Internalizing level, 113
Internally oriented assessment,
63–64
Interpersonal games, 19–31, 149,
199, 206, *207–208*, 209–215. *See
also specific games*

Interrupting games: example illustrating actions taken for, 136–138; knowing the intervention points for, 127–132; to only change the games, problem of, 172–173; steps for, 132–136; in a sustainable way, 138–146

Intervention points, knowing the, 127–132

Intimacy choice, 114–118, 120, 139. *See also* Execution

Invisible links, 149–152

J

"Journey, The" (Oliver), 124

K

Keep Them Guessing game: choosing not to play the, 115; described, 32–33; and executive game playing, 186; and game ecology, 155, 160; impact of the, 53, 57; not confronting the, reasons for, 85; pervasiveness of, reasons for the, 68

Kets de Vries, M., 112, 189

Key principles, 204–205

Kill the Messenger game, 35–36, 77, 86, 154, 161, 186, 199

Knowledge exchange, limiting, 50

L

Labor-management negotiations, 115–118

Labor-management strife, company's history marked by, 157

Leaders, great, traits of, 45, 123–124

Leadership, defined, 123

Leadership from the Inside Out (Cashman), 123

Leadership functions and tasks, effect of games on, 53–61

Leadership games, 31–39, 199, *207–208*, 215–221. *See also specific games*

Leading people, impact of games on, 60

Learning, impact of games on, 49–50

Learning stance, adopting a, 139, 202–203

Let's Not Rock the Boat game, 61, 217

"Level 5 Leadership" (Collins), 45

Lewin, K., 126

Lewis, M., 187

Liar's Poker (Lewis), 187

Locked in Brainstorm game, 223

Love and belonging needs, 109

Lowballed Baseline game, 41–42, 77, 84, 87

M

Machado, A., 205

Machiavellian behavior/attitude, 8, 44, 65, 86

Management Only by Objectives game, 59–60, 216

Manipulation, as a game-playing trait, 15

Marginalize game: and change, 166–167; described, 21–22; and game ecology, 159, 160; impact of the, 50, 54, 59, 60; not confronting the, reasons for, 86, 88; within an organizational context, example of the, 2–3; and organizational evolution,

199; pervasiveness of, reasons
for the, 76
Maslow, A., 109
Maverick (Semler), 117–118
McClelland, D., 84–85
Measuring performance: in a
game-reduced environment,
201, 202; impact of games on,
58–60
MicroStrategy, 223
Mistrusting DNA, 158–159, 163,
168, 169, 171, 173–174. *See also*
Distrustful atmosphere
Modeling, 199
Morale, impact of games on, 50
Morgenstern, O., 12
Mourier, P., 164–165

N

Narcissism, 183–186, 187, 195
Needs: real, identifying, 140, 141;
satisfying, using games for,
67–70, 108; sharing anxieties
and, 114, 138; theory of three,
payoffs from games building
on, 84–87; understanding,
109–110
Negative forces, reducing, while
increasing positive forces,
126–127
Nepotism game, 60, 219
Neumann, J. von, 12
No Bad Feedback game, 59, 110–111,
185–186, 217
No Bad News game: as an
antidote to scapegoating,
181; and awakening, 106; and
the challenge of change, 173;
choosing not to play the,
110–111; described, 28–29; and
the Dilbert cartoon, 198;
and game consciousness, 43;

and game ecology, 154, 155;
impact of the, 54, 59; interrupting
the, 143–144; pervasiveness of,
reasons for the, 76
No Decision game: and the
challenge of change, 174;
described, 33–34; and game
ecology, 154; impact of the, 60,
61; not confronting the, reasons
for, 87; pervasiveness of, reasons
for the, 69, 72, 77, 78
Nonavailability game, 211–212
Not My Problem Anymore game,
217

O

Objective setting, impact of games
on, 58–60
Obsessive DNA, 160–161, 163
Occam's razor, 194
Old War Hero game, 55, 188,
209
Oliver, M., 124
Onboarding, 85
Open and ongoing dialogue:
evolution of an organization
reflecting, 199–202; as a natural
antidote to games, 205; steps
toward, 138–146, 192–194
Opportunistic level, 113
Organizational climate, effect of,
72–73
Organizational culture: diagnostic
for the game-playing aspect
of, 154–156; and game DNA,
166; games as part of the, 2, 6;
prevalence of games based on
type of, 17–18
Organizational environment:
assessing the, 79–82; current
state of the, 47–48; finger-
pointing, 9, 10; game-playing,

V

Vague Big Vision game, 61, 218
Victim game: and the challenge of
    change, 169; described, 24–27;
    and game ecology, 149, 150, 151,
    158, 159, 161; pervasiveness of,
    reasons for the, 75, 77
Virtual environment, effect of a,
    70–71
Vision, fresh, communicating a, 177

W

Wake-up call, emotion serving as
    a, 102–106

Wall Street, 84
Warning signs, 100–102
*What Do You Say After You Say
    Hello?* (Berne), 128
What I Want to Hear game,
    191, 221
Whyte, D., 123
Window Watcher game, 36–37, 74,
    158, 159
World on My Shoulders game,
    58–59, 188–189, 210